LIVE HEALTHY, LIVE WHOLE

"As a physician and doctor of souls, Dr. Carol is uniquely qualified to write this book of knowledge and wisdom. She is well known as a proponent of whole-person health and lifestyle. This book is sure to lead many to wholeness."

—**THOMSEN MATHEW, DMin, EdD,** Dean, College of Theology and Ministry
Oral Roberts University, Tulsa, Oklahoma
Author of *Spirit-led Ministry in the 21st Century*

"Dr. Carol combines wise medical advice with sound biblical principles for healthy living, not just for the body but for soul and spirit. She understands that physical health is closely interconnected with vibrant Christian spirituality, wholesome relationships, emotional wellbeing, and strong marital bonding. *Live Healthy, Live Whole* presents counsel that is both highly practical and solidly biblical."

—**PAUL L. KING, DMin, ThD,** author of *God's Healing Arsenal:
A Divine Battle Plan for Overcoming Distress and Disease*

"Drawing upon her wealth of professional and personal experience, Dr. Carol provides a practical guide to health and wholeness that addresses common areas of life challenges, especially for women. Her emphasis on the integration of physical, relational, and spiritual health enables her to offer hope and guidance to those searching for freedom and well-being. Of special interest to me are her insights regarding the nature of change and her suggestions on finding the motivation/empowerment needed to pursue it."

—**BILL BUKER, DMin, PhD, LPC,** Professor of Counseling,
Oral Roberts University

"Rarely is a nation blessed with a doctor who teaches and reaches out with the Good News while practicing medicine and health care. Dr. Carol is that kind of doctor. Whatever she does in serving, writing, radio or TV, I love and want to experience. Her new book will serve all well in doing that."

—**EVELYN W. DAVISON,** Founder, Love Talk Network
National Day of Prayer Coordinator for Texas

"Some days are like walking on a tight rope across the Grand Canyon without a safety net or a balancing pole. Staying centered and moving forward becomes an incredibly daunting challenge. My friend Dr. Carol helps me understand the fragile balance of body, mind, and soul. In *Live Healthy, Live Whole* Dr. Carol shares from her vast experience and expertise as she helps us align those areas of our lives that will propel us into our destiny. The book is filled with practical, scientific, and scriptural wisdom. It is useful to individuals for self-management as well as for individual and/or group coaching. Read, grow, be enriched, and serve others with wholeness."

—**BRENDA C. CHAND, DMin,** Co-Founder,
Dream Releaser Coaching

"As a life coach I see many people who have created impressive strategies for career success. But those same people frequently leave that appealing plan at risk by having no plan for success in the more foundational physical health, and relationship areas. This entertaining and informative book provides clear methods for being as intentional about success in those areas as in business. Don't take the chance of a successful career and a failed life."

—**DAN MILLER,** New York Times bestselling author
48 Days to the Work You Love

"As you read Dr. Carol's new book I know you will be blessed. I have had the pleasure of working with Dr. Carol for quite some time and her Christian approach to issues of the family and our faith have delighted the readers of our eMagazine. She lives her passion for God in the way she can relate to those of us who need encouragement. She will take you on a great journey."

—**JOANN JORDAN,** Founder,
Garlands of Grace Ministries International

"Dr. Carol once again presents evidence-based knowledge, a commitment to faith, and a splash of good ole common sense in her newest book. A must read!"

—**PHIL ROE, MD,** U.S. Congressman 1st District Tennessee,
Ob-Gyn Physician

LIVE HEALTHY, LIVE WHOLE

Your Prescription for Healthy Living, Loving Relationships, and Joyful Spirituality

Carol Peters-Tanksley, MD, DMin

Live Healthy, Live Whole
Copyright © 2015 by Carol Peters-Tanksley
All rights reserved.

Published in the United States by Credo House Publishers,
a division of Credo Communications, LLC, Grand Rapids, Michigan
www.credohousepublishers.com

Unless otherwise indicated, all Scripture quotations are from The Holy Bible,
New International Version® NIV® Copyright © 1973, 1978, 1984, 2011 by Biblica, Inc.™
Used by permission. All rights reserved worldwide.

Scripture quotations labeled KJV are from the King James Version of the Bible.

ISBN: 978-1-625860-22-4

Cover design by Sharon VanLoozenoord
Interior design by Sharon VanLoozenoord
Editing by Donna L. Huisjen

Names and identifying details have been altered to protect the privacy of individuals mentioned in this book. All stories are true, though on a few occasions a character represents a composite of more than one individual.

Printed in the United States of America

First edition

To my husband, Al.

    I'm the woman I am because of you.

    You are, and always will be,

        the wind beneath my wings.

Contents

Introduction   xi

Part 1: **HEALTHY PERSON**   1
    1 Whole Human Beings: Who Are We?   3
    2 Don't Ignore the Symptoms: A Lifestyle Checkup   9
    3 The Extra Benefits of a Healthy Lifestyle   17
    4 It Isn't All about Me: Your Impact on Others   23
    5 How I Got My Husband to Change   29
    6 Finding Your BIG ENOUGH Reason   35
    7 Addiction: A Total-Person Disease   41
    8 How Your Body Affects Your Mind and Soul   47
    9 It's All in Your Mind: Thinking and Health   53
  10 Learning to Feed Yourself   59
  11 Where Does Healing Begin?   65
  12 What Does "Healthy" Look Like   71

Part 2: **HEALTHY RELATIONSHIPS**   77
  13 How Relationships Affect Your Health   79
  14 Family of Origin: No More Drama   85
  15 When You're Single   91
  16 Red, Yellow, Green: Your Relationship Traffic Light   97
  17 Why Is Sex So Slippery?   103
  18 The Benefits of Healthy Sex Beyond the Bedroom   109
  19 Contraception, STDs, and Other Complications   115
  20 What Makes a Marriage Work?   121
  21 The What and the How of Communication in Marriage   127
  22 When Marriage Doesn't Work: Infidelity and Divorce   133
  23 Do's and Don'ts for Wives on Placing God First   139
  24 Especially for Men: What Women Wish They Knew   145

Part 3: **HEALTHY SPIRITUALITY** 151

    25 Why Spirituality Matters for Your Health   153
    26 Making Scripture Work   159
    27 What Prayer Is All About   165
    28 Sexuality and Spirituality   171
    29 "Unless You Forgive . . ."   177
    30 In Love and War: The Action Part of Love   183
    31 What God Will NOT Do for You   189
    32 "God, Help Me!" Working Together with God   195
    33 What Is Healthy Spirituality?   201
    34 How to Know If Your Faith Is Working   207
    35 "I Am the God Who Heals You"   213
    36 Far into the Future: Eternal Medicine   219

Closing Thoughts   225
About the Author   227
Endnotes   229

Introduction

MARILYN WOULD HAVE preferred to be almost anywhere else that day. She had faced similar medical issues in the past, and the situation had never ended well. She had known the problem might return but had hoped there would be another explanation this time. The physical symptoms were unpleasant, but the fear, anxiety, and guilt were so much worse.

At my first meeting with Marilyn there were plenty of tears. We talked about the results of her ultrasound, and about the minor surgery she would need. She told me about the abuse she had suffered as a teenager, her sexual indiscretions as a young woman, and her strong desire now to become a mother. Her church, her mother, her sister, and her boyfriend all had different ideas about what she should do now, and that confusion only made her anxiety worse.

I sat on my little rolling stool looking across at Marilyn and realizing how anxious, afraid, and even alone she felt. As an OB/GYN physician and Reproductive Endocrinologist there were some important medical issues with which I would help Marilyn, but that was only a small part of what she was dealing with. It would also require my training as a Doctor of Ministry to help her find the clarity and healing she needed.

And it would also require something far beyond what I could provide. Marilyn's relationship challenges, wounded heart, and anxious spirit were even bigger factors in her life and health than the physical issues she faced. Marilyn would need to recognize God's intervention in her life to find the future she was looking for.

There was no magical medical treatment that would cure Marilyn forever. There was no 1-2-3 formula that would make her decisions for her. There was no single Bible verse that would tell her all she needed to know.

But Marilyn didn't expect a simple answer that day, although she would have gratefully accepted one if one had existed. She came for help in putting the medical, emotional, and spiritual aspects of her difficult situation in some kind of perspective. She was looking for someone to show her what she could do to have a happier, healthier future. And so we talked about what medical treatments she would need, how to address her anxiety and fear, and how God wanted healing for her past and joy for her future.

When she left the office that day Marilyn still faced some medical problems. She still had to face the anxiety of the minor surgery she needed. There was no guarantee she would ever get pregnant. And there were things in her past and present she still needed to work through with God and a faith-filled counselor.

But our conversation together did provide her a measure of confidence in knowing what to do next, how the pieces of her life fit together, and that she was not unique or alone. It helped her connect with God at a critically important moment and gave her clarity to take the actions needed right away. Instead of fear and shame, the tears with which she left were tears of relief and hope.

In this book I want to do the same for you. I want to sit on my little rolling stool across from you and put a range of lifestyle, relational, and spiritual issues together for you in a way that makes sense. Not perfect sense, but usable. Meaningful. Manageable. I want to help you see what choices you have and continue to help you through the process of taking action.

I want to help you connect with God right where you need Him.

For more than 20 years I've been privileged to help people in many ways. My medical practice has given me a perspective on some of the most intimate and difficult challenges women face throughout their lifetimes. As a radio host I've talked with people from all over the country about what matters to them, where they hurt, and how hard it is to change. As an ordained Christian minister I've seen God do amazing things in corporate gatherings, through His Word, and in response to heartfelt prayer. I've seen real people with real problems find hope and healing, joy and growth through learning what it means to work together with God.

In this book you won't find all the answers. But you will find help in asking the right questions.

You won't find a magical way to lose weight, find love, or be happy without any effort on your part. But you will know what steps you can take to find the future you desire.

You won't find a promise of miracles. But you will be coached in knowing how to walk with the Miracle Worker.

I saw Marilyn regularly over the next several months. She was relieved at how smoothly her minor surgery went, and physically she is doing well. She is facing her future with much less anxiety and a lot of hope. Just a couple of weeks ago she asked me to pray with her about a specific problem, even as she was taking a scary step toward one of her biggest dreams. She told me she knows God has a good plan for her future, "so I'm turning it over to Him."

I don't know where your biggest challenges are right now. I don't know how hard or long your journey may be. But I do know that your future can be better than your past. I know God has a good plan for you and that you can work together with Him to realize that plan.

This book can be used in a couple of different ways. It can be a great tool to use in a small Bible study group or reading club. At the end of each chapter are questions to talk about, designed to stimulate discussion between you and some friends. You'll get more out of the material if you thoughtfully talk about the issues with others who are also trying to grow.

But beyond that, the most important ingredient of all is your own action. It's almost certain that nothing will be different in your future if you don't change something in your daily life today. That's why there are some suggested action steps at the end of each chapter to help you put the principles talked about into practice. While you will get a lot out of this book just by reading, you'll get a lot more out of it if you follow through on some or many of the suggested action steps.

Think of these action steps as a doctor's prescription. Your doctor can't help you if you refuse to take the pills he or she prescribes! If you thoughtfully work your way through this book you'll have a prescription for moving forward.

And you'll see what it means for YOU to connect with God right where you need Him.

Part One

HEALTHY PERSON

"Dear friend, I pray that you may enjoy good health and that all may go well with you, even as your soul is getting along well." (3 JOHN 2)

*"Tis God gives skill,
But not without men's hands:
He could not make Antonio Stradivari's violins
Without Antonio."* (GEORGE ELIOT)

Chapter 1

Whole Human Beings: Who Are We?

TWO LITTLE GIRLS were walking together to school one beautiful spring morning. They were enjoying the beautiful flowers and the crisp, fresh air. Everything was right with the world as they sang, skipped, chased butterflies, and picked a few flowers.

Suddenly they realized that they had taken so long enjoying the flowers that they were going to be late for school. Soon the bell would ring, and they would be marked tardy. Not wanting to get in trouble, the first little girl said to her friend, "Let's kneel down right here and pray."

"No," her friend answered quickly. "Let's run while we pray!"

I want to help you learn how to run while you pray.

Some people mostly run. We'll call them Group A. They study about health, read food labels, and count calories. They know how many steps (or miles) they walked today and how close they are to their weight goal. Their medicine cabinet is full of vitamins and supplements. They're always looking for a checklist or program to make their home life better. They orchestrate everything in their life and marriage—sex, date night, Bible study, church attendance.

And they're tired. Something still isn't working, no matter how hard they try.

"I know the answer!" says Group B. "You need to pray." Now, it's good to pray. About everything. But praying is about all Group B does. They start with praying for the doctor to find the magic pill to cure them, or the pastor to "fix" their husband. They have lots of problems: multiple medical issues, frequent emotional ups and downs, and a miserable marriage. If only God, or anybody else, would help!

And they're frustrated. Nobody will fix them. Not even God. Sigh.

What's missing? Working harder can't be the answer. If it was, Group A would have it all figured out.

Then why doesn't Group B find the answers? Isn't prayer supposed to fix things?

And so we come to Group C. These individuals know how to both run and pray. They understand that God IS the Answer. They also know they have a role to play. And life just seems to work better for them.

Here's how Jane, a wise member of Group C, looks at her life.

- If she or a member of her family becomes ill, she prays for God's healing. At the same time, she looks at her lifestyle to see if there are any areas in which she has made herself vulnerable. She makes any necessary changes and gets medical care when necessary.

- If she feels anxious or depressed, she spends some extra time listening to what God has to say. She asks her husband for some extra grace and support. She evaluates her life for anything that might have caused her to be overwhelmed and takes appropriate action.

- If she's looking for a husband or unhappy in her marriage, she spends some extra time on her knees. She evaluates how her own attitudes and behavior might be impacting her spouse (or potential spouse). And she studies how good relationships function.

Do you see how that works? There's something about both running AND praying that just makes life work better.

God's View of You

God can and will do amazing things. But He won't take the fork out of your hand to keep you from overeating. He won't make your credit cards disappear to keep you from going further into debt. He won't use the Star Wars magical transponder to "Beam You Up" from work to home to spend time with your family. He values our will enough to generally give us the dignity of our own choices, even if they result in pain.

From the moment God breathed the breath of life into Adam, and fashioned one of Adam's ribs into the beautiful Eve, He created you to be something special. Every part of you is created in His image (Genesis 1:27). And He wants you, He needs you, at your best.

The wonderful creation that's you is a unique, integrated whole. You're not a collection of random parts, like the motor of a car. Separate the pieces of an engine, and each part retains its identity. But you're more like a prize-winning loaf of bread. The ingredients come together in a way that makes them something more than they would be individually. And you can't separate the flour, eggs, and yeast from the bread, can you?

Just so, you can't separate the parts of yourself into completely separate categories. Each one—your physical body, your emotions and thoughts, your relationships with others, and your spiritual being on the inside—is connected to every other. Vitally connected. "Baked" together permanently.

You already know this if you think about it. Have you ever tried to have a deep, meaningful time of prayer with God while struggling with a severe headache? Or how about that knot in your stomach and trouble sleeping after a serious fight with your husband?

The life God makes available to us, and calls us to, involves living healthfully in a physical sense. It involves having a healthy mind and emotions, loving connections with other people, and a strong, vital relationship with God as well.

But in each of those areas there are things for which we must take responsibility. There are times we must run, even while we pray.

And remember that loaf of bread? It's your whole, unique, integrated self that God uses to feed others. It's all the parts of you together, in all their redeemed brokenness and beauty, that become meaningful, useful, and nourishing to other people in God's hands.

I hope you're like the second little girl, both running and praying on her way to school. I hope you become a member of Group C, and experience all its benefits—physically, emotionally, relationally, and spiritually. Throughout the chapters of this book we'll learn how to do just that.

Perhaps an ideal way to begin is with the Serenity Prayer:

> *"God, grant me the serenity to accept the things I cannot change, the courage to change the things I can, and the wisdom to know the difference. Amen."*

It's time to run. And pray.

Suggested Discussion Questions:

1. With which of the three groups do you most identify—A, B, or C? Do you run, pray, or both?

2. Talk about a time when one area of your life affected another (such as a headache affecting your prayer life, or a fight with your spouse making you physically ill).

3. Think about each of the three parts of the Serenity Prayer: serenity, courage, and wisdom. Which aspect do you find the most difficult to experience?

Suggested Action Steps:

1. Make three lists on a piece of paper: (1) the parts of your life that are working well, (2) the parts of your life that aren't working at all, and (3) the parts of your life you want to improve.

2. Can you hone in on one area in which you can "run and pray" this week? What one action can you take, while at the same time praying for God to work in that area of your life?

3. Pray the Serenity Prayer aloud each day this week. In

which area is God working hardest with you? Pause and reflect on your progress in this area.

Scripture to Contemplate or Memorize:

"May God himself, the God of peace, sanctify you through and through. May your whole spirit, soul and body be kept blameless at the coming of our Lord Jesus Christ." (1 Thessalonians 5:23)

Chapter 2

Don't Ignore the Symptoms: A Lifestyle Checkup

I'LL CALL HER Mary.

I could probably use her real name: she's been dead for more than 20 years. I met her one night in the emergency room during my residency training. She had been bleeding for months and finally became so weak that she allowed her family members to bring her to the hospital. She hadn't seen a doctor in years.

The diagnosis was easy to make once I examined her. She had advanced stage cervical cancer. We went through all the medical procedures: blood transfusion, biopsy, X-rays, radiation treatment. We kept her as comfortable as we could. Mary never went home again; she died less than three weeks later, at only 43 years old.

The real tragedy was that Mary didn't have to die. At least not then. Not that way. She could probably have lived for several more decades, enjoying her life and her family, if only . . .

If only she'd received a PAP test at any time during the previous 15 years, the cancer may well have been prevented.

If only she had gone to the doctor when she started bleeding, the cancer could have been treated before it killed her. She could have had a lot more time. And she might even have been cured.

If only she hadn't waited so long, we might have been able to do so much more.

But this isn't really about Mary. It's about YOU.

And it isn't really about PAP tests. It's about the symptoms YOU might be ignoring. Symptoms are a clue that something is wrong. And it might not be what you think.

Symptoms as Useful Information

Symptoms may not always signal what we first think. Chest pain isn't always a heart attack; it might be indigestion. Bloating isn't always ovarian cancer: you might have been eating too much of the wrong food. But you know that if either of those symptoms, or any others, are severe or persistent, you need to get medical attention right away.

It's the same with symptoms in any other area of your life. Wishing, hoping, and ignoring danger signs won't make the problem go away.

And, just as in Mary's case, many problems get worse the longer you put off dealing with them. Spend a little more than what you make each month, and before long you're deeply in debt. Ignore the little problems coming between you and your spouse, and one day you'll hardly know each other. Allow nagging feelings of guilt or bitterness to remain, and soon you'll have lost all your joy—and your Christian experience.

You may have picked up this book because you have a sense that something is wrong somewhere in your life, even if you aren't certain what the problem is. Or you may believe that things should be better and want some help to figure out what to do next. That's what this book will help you do.

All of us would do well to periodically conduct a lifestyle checkup. It's like your yearly checkup with your doctor. (You do go for your yearly exam, don't you?) Think of the questions at the end of this chapter as providing a basic lifestyle checkup. They'll help you to know where to pay closer attention in the chapters ahead.

Referred Pain

In the medical field there's a phenomenon we call referred pain. The place you feel pain may be different from the location from which that pain originates. After abdominal surgery you may feel pain in your shoulders, even though nothing has happened to your shoulders. Pain down the back of your leg may result from a pinched nerve in your lower back.

It's the same way with symptoms in any area of your life. Trouble in one area may show up somewhere else. Feeling guilty about a previous sexual relationship may affect the emotional connection between yourself and your spouse today. Struggling in your attempts to hear God's voice may stem from a brain that's sluggish and tired because of an unhealthy diet. Just because you feel OK in one area is no reason to ignore the questions about that part of your life.

I don't want you to be like Mary. Whatever is going on in your life, don't ignore it. Don't let the cancer—whatever it is—grow unchecked until it kills you. Don't let it drain away the very lifeblood of who you are. Don't ignore the symptoms!

And if you *have* ignored signs of problems in some area, this is your opportunity to wake up. God is a God of new beginnings, and this can be the first day of the rest of your life.

A Lifestyle Checkup

None of us is perfect. God is working on and in each one of us in some area, or perhaps in several. This checklist is designed to help you be more aware of where you are right now, and to see areas in which you can work on growing. We'll talk about many of these topics in upcoming chapters.

Physical and Mental Health

1. Am I taking appropriate care of my body in such areas as eating healthily most of the time and getting appropriate exercise and regular rest?

2. Am I aware of, and doing what I can to address, any physical lifestyle habits God is asking me to adjust?

3. Do I care enough about my body to get appropriate care from medical doctors or other health professionals when I need it, as well as appropriate health screenings from time to time?

4. Where I'm prone to harmful mental patterns such as worry or negativity, am I taking regular action steps to overcome them?

5. Am I able to freely experience the full range of human emotions, both positive and negative: joy, peace, anger, fear, frustration, grief, love, hope? (. . . and the list goes on).

6. Am I choosing my thoughts and attitudes consciously, or working toward doing so more consistently?

7. If I struggle with any addictions, am I doing everything I can to work toward healing in terms of the physical, emotional, and spiritual aspects?

8. Am I being conscious of my media consumption and filtering out programs, websites, or other media that promote ungodly values?

9. Do I spend the majority of my mental energy on things I can change and turn over to God the things I can't?

10. Am I regularly feeding my mind with positive mental food—media promoting positive values, opportunities to learn and grow, Scripture, etc.?

Relational Health

1. Am I able to relate to other people without becoming excessively needy of them?

2. Am I able to open my heart in an appropriate level of intimacy with my spouse and/or with close friends?

3. Have I realistically looked at my family of origin and faced any negative baggage I may have been dragging along?

4. Am I dealing with or expressing my sexuality in a healthy and biblical way, whether I'm married or single?

5. If I'm single, am I focusing most of my energy on becoming the right person rather than on searching for someone to "fix" me?

6. If I'm married, am I working with my spouse to continually improve the intimacy between us, communicate about both superficial and deep things, and fulfill each other's needs?

7. Do I spend most of my time with people who value what I have to offer, who can contribute to my life, or whom I want to resemble?

8. Am I comfortable with my level of unselfishness in my marriage, with my family, and with others?

9. Am I taking appropriate care to have my own needs met so that I'm equipped to offer help to others?

10. Do I experience God working in various ways to bless the lives of others through my life?

Spiritual Health

1. Is my relationship with God solid, resilient, and growing?

2. Is the Bible a regular part of my life, and do I allow its teachings to impact my lifestyle?

3. Do I communicate with God on a regular basis through prayer?

4. Have I worked through the process of forgiving those who've wronged me, either now or in the past?

5. Do I see myself as working together with God to deal with the problems I face, rather than waiting for Him to "do it for me"?

6. Am I open and eager to receive gifts from God, such as healing and divine intervention, wherever God shows up?

7. Can I see my outward behavior increasingly changing as a result of allowing God to work on my inner being? Does sin have less hold on me now than when I first met Jesus?

8. Is my love for God showing itself in action steps to impact my world in a positive way?

9. Is my Christian life reasonably free from distortions such as cheap grace, legalism, or spiritual abuse?

10. To the degree I understand God's purpose for me, am I working together with Him to fulfill that purpose for my life?

So, how did you score? Remember that a checkup is not a test you're supposed to pass. A checkup helps you see where you are now so you can focus your energy in the places you most need help. A checkup helps you notice symptoms before they drain the life out of you, as they did with Mary.

Suggested Discussion Questions:

1. *How do you feel after going through the Lifestyle Checkup?*

2. *Which one (or two) of these questions feels least comfortable to think about? Why might that be so?*

3. *Are you ready to take action in dealing with one area in which you need to change?*

Suggested Action Steps:

1. *Choose one Lifestyle Checkup question that feels uncomfortable.*

2. *Write that question (or key phrases from that question) on a sheet of paper.*

3. *Below that question, answer the following:*

a. *What am I doing now that is healthy in this area?*

b. *What am I doing now (or failing to do) that is NOT healthy in this area?*

c. *What would my life look like if were doing what I already know to be the right course of action in this area?*

Scripture to Contemplate or Memorize:

"Search me, O God, and know my heart; test me and know my anxious thoughts. See if there is any offensive way in me, and lead me in the way everlasting." (Psalm 139:23,24)

Chapter 3

The Extra Benefits of a Healthy Lifestyle

JAMES AND TONIA had been married for nearly 30 years and felt they had a pretty good life. For the last several years they had both been working for a Christian ministry and felt they were making a positive difference in many people's lives.

But their "pretty good" life had problems. Both James and Tonia were dangerously overweight. The problem had been getting worse for years, and it had begun affecting their ability to work, and more. Both of them struggled with significant pain, and James's diabetes wasn't well controlled. They knew something had to change.

A year earlier James and Tonia had made a commitment to live more healthfully. They had joined a weight-loss program and started exercising and eating better. Over a period of nine months they had each lost more than 100 pounds. Wow! They feel so much better physically, but that isn't all. James no longer needs several medications he'd been taking, and Tonia has become even more involved in family, church, and ministry activities that she couldn't do before.

In telling the story Tonia could hardly contain her excitement. As great as the improvement in their physical health had been, the transformation in their relationship was even greater. "Let me put it this way: you certainly don't need Viagra!" she chuckled.

Yes, eating right, getting enough exercise, and not smoking will lessen your risk of heart disease, cancer, and diabetes. You will probably live longer as a result. But is that all?

Lessening your risk of disease and living longer may seem like a boring, unspectacular motivation for maintaining a healthy lifestyle. If that works for you, great. But for many of the rest of us, our lifestyle naturally deteriorates in an unhealthy direction out of habit, convenience, or just plain laziness. You can blame some of that on stress, media, or other factors in our environment. It's the second law of thermodynamics at work again: you must put energy into a system to keep it from degenerating into some variety of chaos.

It may take a crisis to shake you up enough to make the lifestyle changes you need and to stick with them over the long term. If you understand more of the other benefits of healthy living, you may find more of the motivation necessary to actually make those healthy lifestyle choices. And for the record, in this book I'm using the terms "healthy living" and "lifestyle" to refer to much more than your diet and exercise. In fact, we talk only a little about those physical lifestyle factors. We're also referring specifically to your attitudes, your relationships, and your spiritual life—all the little things you do every day that are part of how you live your life.

So here are some of those "other" benefits of a healthy lifestyle. Which of these resonates with you? Living healthier will help you:

1. **Look better.** Especially for women, the vanity factor can be very motivating. Processed food, tobacco, anxiety, and bitterness all age your appearance quickly. A healthy lifestyle can do wonders for your skin, hair, and more. You'll have fewer wrinkles; a brighter, clearer skin color; and shinier, healthier hair. Your eyes will be brighter. You may not even be able to pinpoint why you look better; you just do.

2. **Handle stress better.** Your brain (and your body) needs oxygen, healthy nutrition, and rest. Positive thoughts and emotions provide an important resilience for handling larger problems when they come along. When those necessary elements are present

you may hardly notice many of the normal, everyday stresses of life. And when larger stresses present themselves you'll have much better mental and physical resources available to handle the situation effectively.

3. **Think better.** Your mental efficiency at work, your memory, your ability to learn, your alertness to danger, your ability to make decisions—all of these depend on brain function. And yes, your brain works better when you live healthily. It's that oxygen, nutrition, rest, and positive thinking formula again, minus the "toxins" from bad habits.

4. **Feel happier.** Feeling sluggish, tired, and bloated can take the joy out of an otherwise beautiful day. All those healthy lifestyle habits help you feel better physically. And again, your brain needs that magic formula (oxygen, nutrition, and rest) in order to feel positive emotions. Feeling good mentally and physically creates a positive feedback loop by which you just feel better and better.

5. **Save money.** Being unhealthy can be expensive. More sick days and less energy at work may translate into a lower income and fewer job prospects. And money you spend on doctors, hospitals, and medications, even if you have health insurance, is money you don't have for other things. And think of all the money you don't have to spend on tobacco or other unhealthy habits.

6. **Love better.** Yes, it's true! Lack of physical and emotional vitality from an unhealthy lifestyle can wreak havoc on your sex drive and your ability to enjoy intimacy. A healthy lifestyle gives you an internal sense of well-being that carries directly into the bedroom. And if you're single and looking, more energy and a more radiant glow will make you more attractive to that special someone.

7. **Be more successful.** You can translate the energy, mental sharpness, ability to handle stress, and clearer

emotions that a healthy lifestyle affords into better outward success in almost any endeavor—business, job, family, hobby, ministry. Of course, with greater success you may have to work harder to keep your healthy lifestyle habits going; busy-ness in itself can put many of your new, healthy habits at risk.

8. **Be more spiritually alive.** A healthy lifestyle unclogs the physical brain waves God uses to communicate with us. He honors us when we respect our body as His temple. Spiritual growth is a great initial motivation to develop a healthier lifestyle. And living healthfully will also remove many mental and physical roadblocks and turbocharge your continuing spiritual growth.

Perhaps you think that connecting a healthy lifestyle with spiritual vitality is a stretch. But you already know they're connected, if you think about it. Think about how hard it is to have a deep, meaningful time of prayer with God when you're struggling with a severe headache. God is with you whether you feel good or bad, healthy or unhealthy. But how much stronger your spiritual life can be with a healthy lifestyle.

God cares about your life and health. Eric Liddell (*Chariots of Fire*) expressed it well: "*God made me fast. And when I run, I feel His pleasure.*"

Appreciate the many other benefits of living healthy. Who wouldn't want to take advantage of all this good stuff?

Suggested Discussion Questions

1. *How motivating is "prevent disease and live longer" for you in terms of making healthy lifestyle changes?*

2. *Name three motivators in the everyday lifestyle choices you're making now. Consider issues like physical well-being, family, money, convenience, job, and other people.*

3. *Imagine you were living a perfectly healthy lifestyle. How would it feel? What might be the benefits to you?*

Suggested Action Steps

1. *Consider the eight benefits of a healthy lifestyle listed in this chapter. Which one or two of these areas resonates most with you? Write this down.*

2. *Find a picture that illustrates the lifestyle benefit you would most like to experience. Put that picture on your mirror, refrigerator, or smartphone where you'll see it often.*

3. *Make one lifestyle change this week that you already know will help you experience more of that benefit. For example, adding vegetables to your diet, scheduling a date night with your husband, or signing up for a Bible reading plan email list.*

Scripture to Contemplate or Memorize:

"And if the Spirit of him who raised Jesus from the dead is living in you, he who raised Christ from the dead will also give life to your mortal bodies through his Spirit, who lives in you." (Romans 8:11)

Chapter 4

It Isn't All about Me: Your Impact on Others

CHELSEA HAD JUST turned 40. Something about passing that milestone caused her to pause and look back over the trajectory of her life. The exercise was more than a little depressing. She had spent nearly 10 years in a violent marriage before getting divorced a few years earlier. Now that her ex-husband was in jail, she and her children could breathe a little more easily. Her physical scars had long since healed, but the emotional wounds still made it difficult to even get up in the morning.

But as bad as her own trauma had been, Chelsea could now see danger signs in her children. Her 13-year-old son was getting into physical fights at school and seemed to be angry all the time. Her 10-year-old daughter was already overweight and a frequent victim of bullying. She knew that unless she faced and overcame her own demons, her children were likely to fall into a life of violence, victimization, or both.

Chelsea could name a dozen bad lessons her children had learned from her, such as how to handle difficult emotions, where self-worth comes from, how to be a victim, how to handle stress badly, and the roles men and women play. She was ready to make a change.

The effects of your choices on your own future should be enough to push you to make good decisions today. But your impact on others can be even more sobering.

It may be a little harder to see the impact of your daily decisions on other people. But whoever said "No man [or woman] is an island" had it right.

- Think pornography affects only you? Ask the wife (or husband) whose husband (or wife) has no passion left over for intimacy together.

- Think your anger is only your problem? Ask the son or daughter who never knows what kind of parent will be coming home tonight.

- Think being late to the meeting is your prerogative? Ask the other committee members whose time you've stolen while they've waited for you.

- Think your physically unhealthy lifestyle is making only YOU sick? Ask the employer who doesn't get all you could give. Ask the spouse who worries and watches you destroy your health. Ask the friends or family members who may be robbed of your energy or presence when you check out early.

- Think your bad attitude is no big deal? Ask the coworker who has to constantly put up with your complaining.

- Think your addiction harms nobody but yourself? Ask the child whose dad never shows up for school events. Ask the mom who spends nights lying awake, worrying and praying. Ask the husband whose wife loses all the family money gambling and leaves the bills unpaid.

Your lifestyle affects everyone with whom you come into contact, and many with whom you don't. You may never know the full effect of what you do and how you're living your life today.

And what's true in a negative direction is even truer in the positive. That's what God means when He talks about three and four generations enduring negative effects from one person's sin, but thousands receiving mercy when someone loves and follows God (see Exodus 20:5,6).

- Your smile may be just the thing that gives a stressed-out single mom the courage to do it all again tomorrow.

- Your getting out of debt may change the financial future of your family for generations to come.

- Your integrity when you could have taken the money may give someone else the courage to do the next right thing, even when it's difficult.

- The way you demonstrate love to your spouse may teach your son or daughter how to have a happy and successful marriage.

And that's just the beginning. Your pattern of behavior, the healthy or unhealthy lifestyle you live, your integrity or lack thereof, the way you handle stress—all that and more affects your own family more than you know, and many others you may never know about.

The Gift of Your Transformation

You've heard the expression "Give a man a fish, and you feed him for a day. Teach him to fish for himself, and you feed him for a lifetime." And there's nothing more powerful in teaching someone to fish than seeing YOU do so.

Don't you love stories in which people overcome incredible odds? Bethany Hamilton,[1] surfing again professionally after a shark took one of her arms. Dr. Ben Carson,[2] enjoying a long career as a distinguished pediatric neurosurgeon after a troubled childhood lived in dire poverty. Thomas "Hollywood" Henderson,[3] football legend and drug addict, now clean and sober and creating programs to help youth stay clean. Such stories give you hope that you too can overcome.

That's what I mean by teaching someone to fish by showing them how. You, your life, becomes the best argument for hope in someone else. Whatever problems you overcome, whatever lessons you learn, whatever bad habits you break, whatever positive lifestyle changes you make, whatever maturity you achieve, remember that someone else is watching.

Someone else is struggling with depression. Someone else hates being overweight. Someone else is struggling through a miserable marriage. Someone else is in deep financial trouble. Someone else feels angry, hopeless, afraid, ashamed, or weary. Someone else needs to see you overcome the same problem they're facing right now.

The most powerful thing you can give to someone in trouble is the gift of your own transformation.

Chelsea got some help for her trauma and is now working to develop programs to help other women in trouble, specifically within the church. After some difficult teen years, seeing their mother become a new person gave her children the encouragement they needed to grow past their own problems, and now they're successful, happy adults.

What kind of impact could your life have on those who struggle with the same kinds of problems you've had to overcome?

In the spiritual realm there's no more powerful message for the kingdom of God than a sinner saved by grace who can stand and say, "That was my life back then. But here's my life now, because of what God has done in me!" When one's character backs up those words it creates a message against which even the devil can't argue!

Why not be that inspiration to someone else? Why not allow God to make you a shining example of His transforming grace? Why not take the light you receive, fan it even brighter, and then pass it on?

Your BECOMING will be the best gift you can give to someone coming after you.

Suggested Discussion Questions:

1. *Think of a time when someone else's choice, attitude, or behavior affected you, perhaps without their even knowing it. Share that story.*

2. *Who have you noticed being affected by your behavior? How do you feel about what you now see in them?*

3. *What problem are you overcoming that you hope will help someone else?*

Suggested Action Steps:

1. *Think of someone from whom you've found inspiration. Think about how you can expand that process and pass it along.*

2. *Write down the name of someone (child, spouse, friend, etc.) whom you know has been influenced by your life and identify what your impact on them has been.*

3. *What change in your life do you need to make in view of the other people you impact? Choose one action to take this week in making that change.*

Scripture to Contemplate or Memorize:

"In the same way, let your light shine before men, that they may see your good deeds and praise your Father in heaven." (Matthew 5:16)

Chapter 5

How I Got My Husband to Change

WARNING: READING THIS chapter may create illusions of power and seasons of marital amazement! (You didn't know that was possible, did you?)

My husband, Al, and I were at the doctor's office, seeing his primary care doctor for the first time in several months. After noting his blood pressure and his weight and adjusting his medications, his doctor looked at me and said, "What kind of diet do you have him on? He's doing great."

If you ask Al, he'll tell you he isn't on a diet. He's never skipped a meal, and yet he's lost 85 pounds. Just yesterday he put on a shirt he hasn't worn in five years and was thrilled to see that it fits—loosely. And he's proud to be able to shop for pants off the "normal" rack instead of, as he calls it, the "fat men's store."

But let's go back for a moment. This was a major change! When Al and I first met he was a smoker, and had been for 45 years. He doesn't remember a time when he didn't smoke. He was seriously overweight, and had been for much of his life. He ate, and loved, the typical unhealthy American diet. Breakfast was bacon and eggs, lunch was hamburgers, and a good dinner consisted of fried chicken or spaghetti with meat sauce. He drank nothing but Coke and diet orange soda. Fruits and vegetables—what are those? He was on several medications and was frequently ill.

But all of that changed. No, not in a day or a week, or even a year. It was a long process. Sometimes he felt as though things would never get any better. But the results have been nothing short of amazing.

The first thing Al changed was to stop smoking. That was a huge accomplishment, and it made a big difference in his health right away. It was the toughest change of all. Next came the dietary changes. Now he drinks water most of the time; he has a Coke perhaps every three months. The processed and fried food is gone, and he greatly misses his fruits and vegetables if we don't have them. He's lost 85 pounds simply by eating right. It's been slow, but it's permanent. He's off some of his medications and feels he is healthy enough now to stick around for a while.

Making such major changes isn't easy. Sometimes it was hard for me to watch Al struggle with these adjustments. But it's been so worth it.

How did I get him to change?

Hint: this is where the illusions of power come in! Here's what I did to help my husband accomplish these significant lifestyle changes:

1. **I didn't set out to change him.** People can tell the difference. If you truly love someone first, you MAY be able to help them make a significant change. But that sequence is important. If you try to change someone before or without loving them, they'll dig in their heels and may never change. That holds true for husbands, but also for children, friends, and anyone else.

   And isn't that how God deals with us? He loved us first and only then asks for our allegiance and obedience. Only then does He work to change our behavior.

2. **I tackled things with him that he wanted to change.** I remember exactly where we were sitting, before we were married, when Al asked for my help to stop smoking. I helped him with medication, put up with

his chewing gum, celebrated every new milestone, and bought him snacks when he needed them. He gained a lot of weight at first, and that was tough. Then when he was ready to change his eating habits we worked on that, and the weight started taking care of itself.

If you or anyone else doesn't want to change, not even God can do it for you. A decision, a commitment to change, must come first.

3. **I made it easy(er) for him.** He hated water, so I compromised. I prepared Crystal Light® for him; it was healthier than soda and closer to water. It was a bridge to drinking more healthfully. And when I discovered a healthier food that he liked, I made sure it was always available. I would sometimes help to distract him when he had an urge to smoke. I knew how hard he was working to change and did what I could to help.

Whether it's a physical lifestyle change, an attitude adjustment, or a spiritual practice, change is hard work. Support can sometimes make the difference between success and failure. If you're trying to change something, look for little ways to set yourself up for success.

4. **I helped him focus on the positive.** When he felt bad that his efforts weren't producing better results, I would remind him of how far he'd come. When he became a connoisseur vegetable shopper at the farmer's market, I let him take over that household chore. I would point out the improvements in his physical health, how good he looked in a smaller pair of jeans, or other benefits he was experiencing.

Whether it's you or a loved one who needs to make a change, positive reinforcement throughout the process is important. Look for and focus on the small benefits at every stage along the way.

5. **I always encouraged and never nagged him.** Al will tell you that never once did I nag him about smoking, what

he ate, or losing weight. I believe that was crucial to his success. I became his biggest cheerleader, celebrating every positive change and good result. I tell him often how proud I am of the things he has changed, and that provides wonderful motivation for him to maintain.

We all need to be encouraged. Often. For anyone trying to change, it's a hard enough job already. Don't make that job harder. Remember that God is very patient with you and me. We should be patient too.

Al will tell you that he changed because of me. Perhaps that's true. But he'll also tell you that I never asked him to change. That was his doing, and I'm proud to be his biggest fan.

I tell you that story because Al's lifestyle change has been so dramatic, and so visible. It's one of the best examples I know of how important encouragement is when trying to make an important change.

Let his story encourage you that YOU TOO can make the change you need, whether it's something in your physical lifestyle, in your thinking, in your marriage, or in your spiritual life.

Your decision + action + encouragement + God's grace = transformation.

Suggested Discussion Questions:

1. *What change have you successfully accomplished in the past? What helped you make that change?*

2. *Is there something you'd like to change in your life now? What has kept you from making that change?*

3. *Have you been guilty of trying to get yourself or someone else to change before experiencing or giving love first? How has that worked out?*

Suggested Action Steps:

1. *Write down a time you were successful in making a lifestyle change of some kind, as well as three factors that helped you make that change.*

2. *Write down something you would like to change now and suggest three factors that would make that change easier, or more possible.*

3. *Choose one of those "make easier" ideas you can implement this week, and then do it.*

Scripture to Contemplate or Memorize:

"And we, who with unveiled faces all reflect the Lord's glory, are being transformed into his likeness with ever-increasing glory, which comes from the Lord, who is the Spirit." (2 Corinthians 3:18)

Chapter 6

Finding Your BIG ENOUGH Reason

SHARON HAD SMOKED for more than 15 years. She knew it was unhealthy, but every time she contemplated quitting she found some excuse to put it off. Her husband and most of her friends smoked. Quitting just seemed like too much trouble, even when she found out she was pregnant. She tried to cut down on how many cigarettes she smoked, but often when under stress she'd light up again.

Then Sharon gave birth to a beautiful baby girl. Almost a year later she was having a very bad day and was smoking on the back porch while her daughter played nearby. Lost in thought, she hardly noticed her baby crawling to the edge of the porch. Just in time, Sharon lunged to grab her just as the little girl was about to roll down the stairs. In doing so, the cigarette dropped out of her hand and lightly burned her daughter's arm.

That was the last cigarette Sharon ever smoked. She had found her BIG ENOUGH reason.

Quitting smoking is HARD! Losing weight is HARD! Working to heal a troubled marriage is HARD! Overcoming an addiction is HARD! Changing from a consistently negative attitude to a positive one is HARD!

Any significant change in your habits, patterns of behavior, ways of thinking, or lifestyle is difficult. Your brain is wired to maintain the status quo, even if the consequences of your behavior are painful or destructive. Try to do something different, and your brain throws a full-blown temper tantrum. That's just biology.

Your brain will come up with a thousand reasons to keep doing the same thing over and over again, even if it's terribly unhealthy. Or dangerous. Or even deadly. Call it addiction, habit, or convenience—the only hope of changing is to discover your BIG ENOUGH reason, one that's bigger than the thing you're trying to change.

A Reason Big Enough

Your reason must be big enough to be worth enduring the anxiety, setbacks, difficulty, or even pain you may experience in making a change. Sometimes that reason is positive: an athlete endures the difficult physical training in order to win the race. Sometimes that reason is negative: your spouse is about to leave unless you learn different ways of handling your anger.

We usually respond better to positive reasons for change, but when the problem is severe enough a negative reason will do just fine. In fact, a negative reason may provide the all-important stimulus to start changing, though a positive reason is usually necessary to carry us through the whole change process.

We can't completely stop our brain from screaming when we go against long-standing neurological pathways and attempt a new way of thinking or behaving. Sometimes there's a physical component (such as nicotine addiction) on top of the behavior patterns. Yes, change is HARD!

But that doesn't mean it's impossible. Doing something different will become easier and easier as new pathways are established in your brain. And there are some excitingly helpful ideas that will allow you be more successful at creating those new pathways.

Here are few of those ideas you can implement to help yourself:

1. **Substitute instead of deprive.** If you're trying to quit smokeless tobacco, find something else to put in your mouth. If you're fighting a bad attitude, choose some positive verbal statements instead to say out loud.

2. **Enlist some help.** Telling your friends and family

what you're trying to change and asking for their help will greatly increase your chances of success.

3. **Choose your BIG ENOUGH reason.** There must to be something you want badly enough to go through the anxiety and discomfort of changing a long-standing behavior.

A friend of mine used to say, "When the desire to change exceeds the pain of changing, then you will change."

What Is Your BIG ENOUGH Reason?

How do you find your BIG ENOUGH reason? The answer is as unique as you are. Sharon quit smoking because she realized the habit was hurting the most important thing in the world to her—her daughter. Your BIG ENOUGH reason needs to be one that engages your intellect, your will, and your emotions. It's the thing you can't imagine living life without.

Here are some categories of reasons that may be BIG ENOUGH:

1. **You're sick and tired of the way things are.** When you get angry enough at being broke, sad, or sick, this can be enough motivation for some people. You cut up your credit cards because you're determined to get out of debt. You drastically change your eating habits because you can't stand being tired and overweight for one more day. Simply being unhappy with your current state of affairs isn't enough: you need the emotional fuel of becoming angry enough at your current situation to take drastic action in a positive direction.

2. **You care about someone else.** My husband's son quit smokeless tobacco because he didn't want his own young son to learn the habit from him. You may see how your bad attitude is hurting your children or your spouse. You may realize that your lack of health is negatively impacting your marriage. You may care enough about someone else to permanently change your behavior.

3. **You want a different future.** Perhaps you've watched a parent die of diabetes or heart disease, and you don't want to repeat that. Or you value your marriage enough to change the way you handle conflict and work to create a new relationship together. You realize that your current behaviors won't give you the outcome you want, and you crave a different future badly enough to change.

4. **Your heart is changed.** I believe this is the biggest BIG ENOUGH reason of all. This is where God can make such a difference. He works a major change in your heart, and you become willing to endure whatever it takes to work out that change in your daily life. You're different on the inside, and all the outside stuff changes as a result. God supplies the courage and wisdom to create a whole new lifestyle in whatever area you give Him control.

In the last chapter you read about how I watched my husband, Al, struggle to overcome tobacco addiction. He knew all the negative health consequences. He had even watched a good friend die from the respiratory effects of smoking. And he himself had developed some serious health problems as a result of the addiction.

But he kept on smoking.

Then we got married, and he quit. It was hard. But he hasn't had a cigarette since. If you ask him why, he'll tell you that he finally had a big enough reason to quit. He wanted to stay alive to enjoy life with me for as long as possible. And that gave him the motivation to go through the very difficult process of change.

Don't say "I can't." Find your BIG ENOUGH reason. Get angry enough at your current state of affairs to change. Give God permission to change you on the inside. Your future awaits.

What's your BIG ENOUGH reason?

Suggested Discussion Questions:

1. *Think about difficult things you've accomplished in the past. Do you respond better to positive or negative motivation?*

2. *Can you think of a BIG ENOUGH reason to change that grabs your intellect, will, and emotions? How do those aspects of your mind work together?*

3. *Is there some part of your heart and life you feel God pulling on you to change? How open do you think you are to letting Him change you on the inside?*

Suggested Action Steps:

1. *If you already know your BIG ENOUGH reason, write it down. Try writing it from both a negative and a positive perspective.*

    a. *If I DON'T change, . . .*

    b. *If I DO change, . . .*

2. *Tell a trusted friend or family member what you want to change, and why. Ask for their encouragement and help.*

3. *Choose something that reminds you of your BIG ENOUGH reason: a picture of a loved one, a doctor's report, a portion of Scripture. Place it somewhere where you will see it often.*

Scripture to Contemplate or Memorize:

"Therefore, if anyone is in Christ, he is a new creation; the old has gone, the new has come!" (2 Corinthians 5:17)

Chapter 7

Addiction: A Total Person Disease

JAMES'S LIFE HAD been rocky right from the start. His parents were on again, off again in their marriage, and then his dad died unexpectedly when James was 12. With his mom's encouragement and support James did fairly well for a while. He was a bright enough student and started college, but soon he began drinking and partying. The loss of his father continued to eat away at his insides. Within a year he was on the street drinking, using drugs, and going downhill fast.

From the moment we enter this world stuff happens, and we're all affected in some way. We get hurt, and we respond in various ways just to survive. We make choices, some good and some not so good.

You may do any number of things to survive the stuff happening to and around you. Your brain desperately wants to feel better, and the things you do change various brain chemicals along the way. What happens in your brain is quite similar (though not identical) regardless of what you use to medicate or self-medicate: illegal drugs, prescription drugs, pornography, gambling, sex, over- or under-eating, and many other possibilities. As time goes on it takes more and more of the substance or behavior to create the same good feeling. And you're hooked. That's an overly simplistic picture of the onset of an addiction, but it's almost always accurate to some degree.

The numbers concerning addiction are truly staggering. Nearly 25 million Americans used illegal drugs last year.[1] Another 15 million abuse prescription drugs. About 18 million have an alcohol use disorder.[2] In the US 2.8 billion dollars is spent every year on pornography.[3] One third of all internet downloads are pornographic.

And the problem is huge among Christians as well. Among Christian young people, 45% self-report having tried marijuana.[4] In addition, 50% of Christian men and 20% of Christian women report being "addicted" to pornography.[5] These numbers should sober us as individuals, as a society, and as a church.

But enough of statistics. If addiction is your struggle, you know the most about the personal devastation it causes. Children going without food. Innocent people killed by drunk drivers. Homes, businesses, and careers lost. Men, women, and children abused physically, sexually, and mentally. Families and lives devastated.

In this brief chapter we can't address the complete anatomy of an addiction, or every aspect of the journey to healing and recovery. But we can show how any addiction impacts every possible component of one's life. And that means that recovery must include all those components as well.

Is Addiction a Disease?

In recent years a push has been made in psychological and medical circles to consider addiction a disease. This makes for an interesting debate, and I'm not going to definitively settle that question here. Calling addiction a disease does emphasize some realities that are true:

- Addiction is not weakness. You don't wake up one day and decide to become an addict.

- Addiction is stronger than you are. Whatever it is you're addicted to takes over your life, and you're powerless to get rid of it on your own. It becomes more important than your health, your family, or even your life.

- Addiction changes you. The physical, biological, and genetic aspects of addiction are real. And it affects you in every part of your life—physically, mentally, emotionally, relationally, financially, and spiritually.

But calling addiction a disease also creates a big problem. That concept can suggest that you aren't responsible for your addictive behavior. That may not be what many people who use this terminology are trying to convey, but it's easy to take it that way. If you struggle with an addiction you may have to take extraordinary measures to behave differently. You may have to get special help and make *permanent* changes in your lifestyle that someone else may not have to make.

But YOU are responsible to take those measures. Genetics plays a role in many addictions, but if you're one of the individuals affected in this way that only means that addiction is one of the challenges you may have to face. Someone else may have a wholly different set of challenges. Nothing gives you an excuse to let addiction take over your life forever.

Rather than referring to addiction as a disease, I prefer to call it a symptom. Some addictions are more destructive or have a greater biologic component than others, but this is only a matter of degree. The process in the brain is remarkably similar for most addictions.

If addiction is a symptom, what is it a symptom of? It's a symptom of brokenness. It's the manner in which our human nature tries to survive in the midst of overwhelming needs that aren't getting met in any other way. It's a way to cover up pain and emptiness. When addicts leave behind one addiction—say alcohol or nicotine—it's easy for them just to run to another one—like food.

Moving to a less-destructive addiction may be better than doing nothing at all. But all addictions end in destruction. Learning to live addiction-free in every area of your life may be the biggest challenge you'll ever face. It may be the hardest thing you've ever done, and it may take every bit of internal strength you have, along with some you never thought you could find. But it IS possible. And you're the only one who can take the necessary steps to find that freedom.

Spiritual Healing from Addiction

If you're addicted, the most devastating cost of all is to your soul. You may face overwhelming guilt, separation from God and others, and fear of hell, and you may feel powerless to do anything to break free.

There's no more obvious example of a soul problem that infects everything else in your life. Your physical health is ruined, your mind held captive, your finances depleted, your relationships devastated, and your soul left bankrupt. Dealing only with the outward issues won't bring the heart change you need in order to be truly free.

Sounds pretty dire when you look at it like that, doesn't it? Yes, addiction is powerful. It's one of the enemy's most successful tools to bring pain and destruction to God's children.

But as powerful as addiction is, there is One who is more powerful. Jesus Himself is the Bondage Breaker. He has already gone to hell and back for you, and He offers you a way out.

If you're struggling with an addiction yourself, let me offer you the hand of Jesus, and, through Him, the hand of others who love Him. Because the roots of addiction are in your soul, allowing God to deal with your heart is the only certain way to find lasting freedom.

And if you're praying for a loved one caught in an addiction, let me also offer you the hand of Jesus, and of others who love Him. You aren't alone in your prayers. So never give up. Perhaps God will use you to be His human hands in helping your loved one and others find freedom.

James made the choice to enter rehab, and now, four years later, he's counseling other recovering addicts. He has dealt with the pain of losing his father and now feels happier and healthier than ever. He celebrates helping others find freedom in the same way he did.

And you can too.

Suggested Discussion Questions:

1. *Identify some of the "stuff" that may lead someone to become addicted.*

2. *What are some of the ways in which addiction infects every area of a person's life?*

3. *Do you see any signs of addiction in your own life? What emotions does that question bring up in you?*

Suggested Action Steps:

1. *If you see any signs of addiction in your own life,*

write down a list of factors that are keeping you from seeking help.

2. *Ask a Christian friend to pray with you for God's courage and strength to take the steps you need in order to become free.*

3. *Find a Celebrate Recovery[6] (or other similar group) in your area. Go to the next meeting.*

Scripture to Contemplate or Memorize:

"Now the Lord is the Spirit, and where the Spirit of the Lord is, there is freedom." (2 Corinthians 3:17)

Chapter 8

How Your Body Affects Your Mind and Soul

JESSICA AND HAROLD seemed like a happy couple. They had become part of a church family shortly after getting married and were excited about the spiritual growth they were experiencing. Over the next few years they became active in many aspects of church work, and young Christians often sought out Jessica for her insights and encouragement.

Then somewhere around the birth of their second child things changed. Previously outgoing and cheerful, Jessica became anxious and depressed. She was afraid to leave the house without Harold and could barely make it through a normal day of childcare. Lack of sleep, weight gain, pelvic pain, doctor visits, medications—her life was a mess. Harold hardly knew the woman Jessica had become, and he struggled to remain engaged with her. Gone was the church work and encouraging other young Christians. If asked, Jessica would say she wasn't even sure God cared any longer.

Stories like Jessica's demonstrate how the many aspects of our lives are interconnected. For Jessica, the hormonal changes and physical pain after childbirth triggered serious mental/emotional problems, put her marriage on hold, and seemed to make connecting with God all but impossible.

We live in a physical world. Our bodies are affected by our environment, genetics, lifestyle habits, and more. Our physical health affects our mental/emotional well-being, our ability to engage in healthy relationships, and the quality of our spiritual growth. Even if you don't consider your physical health to be all that important right now, taking care of your body will impact every other aspect of your life.

If you think about this, you'll realize that you already know it. Have you experienced any of the following "small" moments?

- You get angry at your child over a minor mistake after you've been up much of the night.

- Your husband knows when he should avoid suggesting intimacy because you're "hormonal."

- You pass on an opportunity to join some friends in a ministry project because you don't have the energy.

- Your prayer time feels nearly nonexistent because of a persistent headache.

The quality of your physical health IS impacting the rest of your life, whether or not you want it to. Your finances, your ability to handle stress, the quality of your relationships, your ability to hear God's voice—all of this and more is affected when your body isn't functioning at its best.

Let's pause here for a moment. The fact that we're human means that weakness, sickness, and death will be a part of our living in this world. We can't expect a body that isn't impacted by imperfections, vulnerabilities, and the effects of aging. There are many examples of people who have overcome serious physical limitations to make an enormous positive impact on those around them and in the kingdom of God. God understands our physical limitations. "He remembers that we are dust" (Psalm 103:14).

The point isn't for us to feel guilty over a less than perfect body. The point is to realize that our bodies, though imperfect, are important. How we care for them makes a difference not only to us but to others around us and, even more importantly, to God.

Evidence That Physical Health Matters

It's no surprise to medical researchers that physical health impacts all other areas of life. Mood disorders such as depression are much more common among those with medical illnesses.[1] Among patients visiting a primary care doctor for a medical problem, 29% of them had significant depression or anxiety symptoms as well.[2] There are numerous studies documenting the mental health impacts of heart disease[3], cancer[4], diabetes[5], back pain[6], and many other illnesses.

Space doesn't permit us to fully explore how your physical health impacts your relationships, your financial health, and your happiness in general. I think you can already see those connections.

But we do need to talk about why you as a Christian should care about your physical health. You're not taking your body with you to heaven, so why worry about it?

Your physical health matters in your Christian life more than you may realize. Here are some specific ways your spiritual life is positively impacted when you care for your body well:

1. **You're more effective.** God can and does use anyone, healthy or not, who will allow Him to do so. But whatever God has given you to do you can do so more efficiently and effectively with a body that's healthy and strong.

2. **You're a positive advertisement for God's kingdom.** Who are you more likely to want to be like: someone who is angry, sick, tired, and miserable, or someone who is positive, energetic, kind, and healthy? Remember that you're the only gospel some people will ever read.

3. **You hear God's voice better.** Having a brain that is clear, healthy, alert, and not clogged with toxins puts you in a much better position to understand God's Word and to hear His voice when He speaks to you.

4. **You experience God's restoration now.** Sin broke everything about us, our physical health included. Working together with God to maximize your

physical health allows much of His restoring power to work in you here and now (Romans 8:11).

5. **You worship God when you care for your body.** God created you in His image, and He re-created you again in saving you. He deserves and asks for your worship in return. Presenting your whole being to Him in worship involves caring for your physical body (Romans 12:1,2).

Your physical health isn't important enough to be a "god" in itself. But it IS important because of the difference it makes in every other aspect of your life.

And hey, you want to feel better too, don't you?

Yes, your physical health makes a difference in every other part of your life, including your spiritual connection with God. Perhaps that can become your BIG ENOUGH reason to make any necessary adjustments in your physical lifestyle.

Suggested Discussion Questions:

1. *How do you feel about your physical body? Love it? Hate it? Ignore it? Why do you think you feel that way?*

2. *How do you think the state of your physical health is affecting the people closest to you, as well as the kingdom of God?*

3. *What do you think God thinks about your physical health? Does it really matter to Him?*

Suggested Action Steps:

1. *Write down three words or phrases that describe the degree of value you attribute and the care you devote to your physical body. On the negative side, you might write things like "Too hard to change" or "Don't care enough."*

2. *What do you think is your biggest roadblock to being*

physically healthier? Knowing what to do? A negative environment? Lack of support? Try to be realistic.

3. *Write down something over which you DO have a choice related to your physical health? It might be "Get a physical checkup" or "Plan my food shopping better." Follow through on that prompt this week.*

Scripture to Contemplate or Memorize:

"Therefore, I urge you, brothers, in view of God's mercy, to offer your bodies as living sacrifices, holy and pleasing to God—this is your spiritual act of worship" (Romans 12:1).

Chapter 9

It's All in Your Mind: Thinking and Health

POPULAR CHRISTIAN AUTHOR and speaker Joyce Meyer is known for her frequent emphasis on our thought life. She openly tells her story of growing up in an abusive and troubled home, revealing that even after becoming a born-again Christian she struggled with negative thinking.

> *I had encountered so many disappointments in life—so many devastating things had happened to me—that I was afraid to believe that anything good might happen. I had a terribly negative outlook on everything. Since my thoughts were all negative, so was my mouth; therefore, so was my life.*
>
> *When I really began to study the Word and to trust God to restore me, one of the first things I realized was that the negativism had to go.*[1]

Joyce Meyer is an example of someone who worked with God to completely change her thought patterns, not only in the area of negative thinking but in many other ways as well. And as a result her life was changed, so much so that she has had a huge positive impact for the kingdom of God.

We don't often think about our thinking. We encounter thousands of messages every day—from media, other people, and many other sources. Many of those messages are negative. In response a thought comes along, and it turns into a feeling. We hold on to that feeling, and it takes over our behavior. Our thoughts impact our physical health, our relationships, our success in every other area of life, and our relationship with God.

Scientists continue to discover more about how our mental/emotional state impacts our physical health. Here are just a few of those connections:

- How one responds to stress impacts one's risk of developing cancer[2], as well as the risk of that cancer spreading.[3]

- People with a Type D personality (negative outlook, worry, gloom) have a higher risk for heart disease than those with a more positive outlook.[4]

- At least one third of individuals with long-term pelvic or gastrointestinal pain report having experienced sexual or physical abuse in the past.[5]

You may think of your thoughts and emotions as intangible and "all in your mind." But thoughts create chemical and electrical signals in the brain that spread throughout your whole body via nerves and blood vessels. Almost every body system is affected by these chemicals and signals. Your thoughts happen "all in your head," but their effects don't stop there.

Anxiety and bitterness are only two specific examples of how what goes on in your mind affects your health as a whole.

Anxiety

Most people feel anxious at times, either about something specific or about life in general. This "fight or flight" response your body experiences under stress is normal. But when you feel anxious most of the time your body produces stress chemicals continually, and that can lead to all kinds of physical symptoms. Over time this can cause real damage.

Anxiety is a common problem for which people seek medical care. They may go to the doctor for symptoms such as headaches, stomach pain, or insomnia, but the underlying reason for those symptoms is anxiety.[6]

Anti-anxiety medication may help you feel calmer, but the physical changes anxiety produces may still continue. It's better to take the time to learn healthier ways of thinking and better ways of managing stress. Dealing with the underlying causes for anxiety will help you be physically healthier, mentally happier, and more spiritually alive.

Bitterness and Lack of Forgiveness

There isn't a person anywhere who hasn't had something bad happen to them and who couldn't reasonably be bitter as a result. But holding a grudge doesn't do anything to harm the one who hurt you; it only hurts *you*.

Lack of forgiveness is toxic. While we've heard that from preachers, we need to hear it more regularly from doctors. Among other negative effects, an unforgiving attitude may lead to high blood pressure, an unhealthy cholesterol balance, and decreased coronary blood flow.[7] Learning to forgive can actually improve the blood flow in those coronary arteries.[8] Ongoing bitterness has also been associated with immune problems, chronic pain, and possibly cancer, not to mention how bad it is for your emotions and your soul.

We'll talk more about forgiveness in chapter 29. For now, realize how important it is to your health. Forgiveness isn't a feeling, but it can certainly result in feelings. Forgiveness includes acknowledging how you were hurt, choosing to let the other person (or people, or yourself!) off the hook, and living for the future instead of the past. It takes time, and God's grace, to forgive well.

Thinking Right

We live in a world where there are problems. And the negative thoughts and emotions we encounter often seem beyond our ability to control. So what does a biblical, godly thought life look like?

What it is NOT:	What it IS:
1. Mind over matter 2. Ignoring negative realities 3. Letting emotions rule you 4. Letting negative issues take your focus	1. Taking your thoughts captive (See 2 Corinthians 10:4) 2. Choosing HOW you deal with negative facts 3. Using emotions as a tool to give you information 4. Choosing to focus on what you CAN do

Positive thoughts may not automatically cause good things to happen. But you do have much more control over your thoughts and attitudes than you realize. God gave you the ability to choose what you think about.

I didn't always understand that I could take charge of my thinking. As a young woman I lived for many years with enormous emotional pain, and I had to learn the hard way how to develop new thinking habits. It's a choice, but it does get easier the longer you do it.

Sometimes I still cry. Sometimes I get angry. Sometimes I feel small, . . . but at other times I feel as though I could take on the world. There's a time for everything, including both positive and negative feelings (Ecclesiastes 3:1–8).

The important thing is to learn how to make your feelings follow your thoughts instead of allowing emotions to lead you around.

Here are some techniques that can help:

- **Consider your physical lifestyle.** Proper sleep, exercise, and a healthy diet have a significant impact on brain function. A rested, properly nourished mind is much happier and more focused.

- **Choose your thoughts.** When you're facing a difficult circumstance or negative feeling, pause. Just STOP. That interruption will help you make a conscious choice about what to think or do next.

- **Get help when needed.** If you aren't making progress on your own, seek out a pastor, counselor, or mental health professional who respects and values your faith and can help you incorporate that into your recovery. And medication has a place. Just don't use it as a substitute for the physical, mental, and spiritual work you need to do.

- **Pay attention to your environment.** Your mental diet makes a difference in your thinking. Spend time around people who are encouraging and faith-filled. Make sure the media you consume provides the kind of nourishment you want your mind to consume.

- **Let God's Word transform your mind.** God's Word is powerful to help you develop new thought patterns. It's one of the most powerful weapons available to counteract the harmful thoughts and messages that bombard you every day.

You have much more control over your thoughts than you realize. I learned that. Joyce Meyer learned that. You can learn it too.

Suggested Discussion Questions:

1. *How much control do you have over your thoughts? Over your attitudes?*

2. *What is your biggest attitude challenge: Being anxious? Negative? Bitter? Hopeless? Angry?*

3. *Share a negative emotion or circumstance that causes you to have difficulty maintaining a good attitude. Let others offer you suggestions on how you can think about the issue more hopefully.*

Suggested Action Steps:

1. *Write down 20 good things you could choose to think about (such as troubles you've overcome or people who care about you).*[9]

2. *Write down (or bookmark in your Bible app) at least*

three Scripture passages that specifically counteract negative thoughts with which you may be struggling.

3. *For the next week, each morning and each evening look at your list and Scriptures and choose one positive thing to think about for 10 minutes.*

Scripture to Contemplate or Memorize:

"Finally, brothers, whatever is true, whatever is noble, whatever is right, whatever is pure, whatever is lovely, whatever is admirable—if anything is excellent or praiseworthy—think about such things." (Philippians 4:8)

Chapter 10

Learning to Feed Yourself

ANGIE COULDN'T UNDERSTAND why she always felt so unhappy. Many things about her life seemed perfect. Her part-time job was interesting, and her teenage daughter was doing well in school. Her husband, Mike, provided adequately for their financial needs. No one in the family had any serious health problems.

But something was definitely wrong. Angie's unhappiness was only getting worse. Mike truly cared about his wife and was honestly trying to help. For his part, Mike felt as though he was giving Angie everything she asked for but that it was never enough. The more he did, the more she wanted. "I feel like I'm dealing with a bottomless pit. Nothing will satisfy her!" he complained.

When children are very small they need to be fed. Someone else makes all the decisions for them, including what, when, and how much they'll eat. Learning to feed themselves is an important milestone of growing up that most children enjoy.

Your body still needs food on a regular basis. But now that you're grown up, you make your own choices about what, when, and how much to eat. Your mind, soul, and spirit need nourishment too. You need a regular diet that includes mental stimulation, entertainment, perspective, feedback, humor, refreshment, communication, intimacy, encouragement, challenge, hope, meaning, depth, joy, love, and worship. When you don't experience enough soul nourishment you go looking. And it's in the looking that you can get into trouble.

Twelve-step programs have a maxim that illustrates this: Don't get too **H**ungry, **A**ngry, **L**onely, or **T**ired. **HALT**—when these needs aren't being met, you're in danger. Your thinking gets cloudy, and you can easily reach for an unhealthy addiction.

Sometimes a mental fast-food snack will keep your soul's hunger at bay for a time. But as is the case with physical food, that satisfaction tends to be short-lived and is often unhealthy. You regularly need some high-quality nourishment for the deeper parts of you. Neglect doing so for too long, and you'll become irritable, short-sighted, frustrated, angry, and ineffective. You can easily turn to dangerous or unhealthy behaviors you'll later regret. Expecting any person besides yourself to meet all your needs and fill your soul indefinitely will only lead to disappointment.

Angie has been looking to her husband Mike to "feed" her for a long time in ways he can't fulfill. Just as in learning to feed herself with physical food, Angie will need some practice in order to learn to feed herself emotionally and spiritually. But doing so is the only way in which she'll be able to feel happy again.

Ways to Feed Yourself

There are many ways to give your soul some gourmet nourishment. You may already know what fills you up and simply need to feed yourself on a more regular basis. But if you're feeling internally empty and need some ideas on where to find some nutritious soul food, here are some possibilities:

1. **Spend time with nature.** Take an hour, an afternoon, or a weekend to disconnect from your digital life and experience the natural. Watch a flock of birds flying, or geese on a lake. Plant some flowers. Sit and listen to a stream gurgling, or to the rush of ocean waves. Hike to the top of a mountain, or ride a horse across the pasture. Go outside at night and gaze at the stars; drive out of town if you need to.

Nature reminds you that God is bigger than you are, that there's beauty in the world, and that your problems aren't so overwhelming after all. It's healing, calming, restoring.

2. **Choose what enters your mind.** Information, entertainment, music, internet sites, books, or magazines can either drain you or fill you. Try consciously choosing what enters your eyes and ears. Play music in your home instead of the TV. Go to a concert. Play the piano, or another instrument. Consciously enter the emotion of the music during your church service. Sign up for some spiritually nourishing email lists. Check out the library, podcast lists, or your Christian bookstore.[1]

   The right music and other input will lift you up and put you in a great mental/spiritual place. Such uplifting input will not only satisfy but stretch and strengthen your inner being.

3. **Connect with positive people.** Negative, needy, or selfish people will drain you. Positive, healthy, and generous people help fill you up. Find someone with a positive outlook on life to talk with and just be around. Perhaps it's a sister, a classmate, a coworker, an old friend, a neighbor, or a church member. Get together and share what's good and bad in your life, and what God is doing for you. Listen as they share in the same way with you. (Hint: positive people have learned how to feed their own soul and hence have much to pass on.)

   No man (and that includes women!) is an island. God created us to be connected. Different personalities connect differently, but don't isolate. Connection makes you stronger.

4. **Do something good for someone else.** Stretch yourself a little. Do something generous not because you have to but simply to give of yourself. Visit your mom

and dad, listen to their stories, and cook a meal for them. Volunteer at the Salvation Army, Red Cross, or a homeless shelter. Make a single mom's day by volunteering to watch her children for a few hours. Be a big sister, or teach literacy at your local library.

Reaching beyond yourself is guaranteed to lift your spirits. There are people with problems much bigger than yours. You'll come away feeling more blessed on the basis of the help you give.

5. **Look to God for what only He can provide.** Scripture isn't just for study; it's for spiritual food. Sit down in a quiet place, ask God to be with you, and open your Bible. If you don't know where to begin, start with the Gospels or the Psalms. Read for a little while, and when you sense a word, verse, or passage speaking to your soul, stop there. Talk to God about it, and then be quiet and wait. It may feel uncomfortable to be silent at first, but do it anyway. Trying to fill your need for spiritual meaning with physical things or human interaction will always leave you empty in the end. There are some ways in which only God Himself can fill you up.

God's food is the best of all. Being still allows Him and His Word to nourish your soul like nothing else can, and to truly transform your inner being.

HALT! Don't let your soul go hungry. Don't wait for someone else to meet your needs. You may have another favorite way to find nourishment. Just be sure you do so often.

Take responsibility for taking in nourishment for your soul before emptiness makes you do something you'll regret.

Suggested Discussion Questions:

1. *How Hungry, Angry, Lonely, or Tired are you? Are there other signals that let you know you're internally empty?*

2. *What are some of the unhealthy ways in which you've tried to feed yourself?*

3. *Share two or three specific ways you've found to nourish your inner being.*

Suggested Action Steps:

1. *Make two columns on a piece of paper. In the first, list all the things you can think of that drain you. In the second, list the things that fill you up.*

2. *Look at your lists. Which draining elements can you lessen or eliminate? Which filling elements can you do more of?*

3. *From your list of things that fill you up, choose one and follow through with it this week.*

Scripture to Contemplate or Memorize:

"The LORD will guide you always; he will satisfy your needs in a sun-scorched land and will strengthen your frame. You will be like a well-watered garden, like a spring whose waters never fail." (Isaiah 58:11)

Chapter 11

Where Does Healing Begin?

SAMANTHA CAME TO see me for help in trying to get pregnant. She and her husband had been trying to have a baby for three years, and she had just now worked up the courage to seek medical help. She wasn't very hopeful and anticipated hearing bad news. She had also suffered with pelvic pain for years, and it had been increasing recently. Now the pain and the stress of trying to get pregnant were making intimacy with her husband almost impossible, which was understandably causing problems in their relationship.

Samantha's home life as a child had been chaotic and abusive. She had tried as a teen to escape through numerous sexual relationships and had experienced both repeated STDs and an unplanned pregnancy that ended in an abortion. She struggled with guilt and anxiety and wondered if she was doomed to forever live with infertility as a punishment for her past.

Most of us, like Samantha, come through life with a bundle of scars. Some of those scars are inflicted on us from the outside by people who don't care, don't know any better, or act in consciously evil ways. Some are inflicted by tragic life experiences, by accidents in our genes, or by other negative circumstances beyond our control:

poverty, abuse, lack of education, racism, and the list could go on. We're beaten up badly in this world.

But that isn't the worst of it. Often our most disfiguring scars are those we inflict upon ourselves. Our responses to the traumas we experience often add to our wounds. Our drives for relief, connection, adventure, meaning, and even basic survival lead us to self-destruct inch by inch. Looking back, could we have done any better? It may be nearly impossible to determine where the fault of other people ends and our own responsibility begins.

The bottom line is that you're broken. I'm broken. Each of us is a strange mix of beauty and ugliness, strength and powerlessness, brilliance and stupidity. And regardless of how hard we try, we can only go so far in fixing ourselves. We need healing—healing from the scars inflicted on us and healing from the scars we inflict on ourselves.

But how do you find that healing? As a doctor, I can give you pills. I can recommend changes in your lifestyle that can improve your health. I can do surgery at times. Once in a while I might even save someone's life. But can I heal you?

As someone wanting to be physically healthy, you might get all the exercise you need. You might follow healthy eating habits, get enough sleep, and take plenty of vitamins. But will that heal you?

You might seek help from a psychologist, self-help group, naturopath, lifestyle coach, or some other professional. You may learn a lot, and you'll probably feel much better. But will that heal you?

As a minister, I can pray for you. I can teach you about having a relationship with God, and about faith. I can introduce you to Him and help bring you into His presence. But can I heal you?

Any picture of health, wholeness, and healing must take into account the full spectrum of interconnected brokenness we experience. And with such deep wounds, God is the only Source of true healing for where we hurt.

What does healing look like?

God is after your total transformation. He wants you whole. Sometimes He reaches out with a dramatic healing touch in a moment, and your pain or problem is gone. It's appropriate to rejoice at those moments. Hallelujah! But that's only one part of the package.

Healing involves every part of you. Healing would look like:

- Your body strong, free of pain and disease, functioning at its best
- Your mind clear, free from addiction, confusion, anxiety, and fear
- Your emotions resilient, able to experience joy, wonder, peace, and hope
- Your finances sufficient, your vocation meaningful
- Your relationships satisfying, real, rich, and full of love
- Your spirit alive, free of guilt and shame, connected with God
- Your character mature, living with courage, generosity, and faith

Wow! That sounds impossible, doesn't it? And so we too often settle for our addictions and short-term fixes, at best lessening our dysfunction for a little while, even though God is after our total healing. That's why you need Him so desperately in this process.

What will healing look like for Samantha? Sometimes medical treatment can make a significant difference. Perhaps through surgery Samantha's pelvic pain will improve, and that may allow her relationship with her husband to improve. Perhaps she'll be able to receive his love more fully, both physically and emotionally, and that may help them together realize their hope of having a child. Or perhaps through other medical treatment she'll become pregnant, and the joy of a baby will help heal much of the pain in her soul.

But simply addressing one area without allowing oneself to experience fuller healing in all other areas may make some issues even worse. If Samantha has a baby but her marriage isn't healed, the loving home she hoped to build may not even be there to bring that child into. To cite another example, someone who experiences a healing from back and knee pain may soon be back in the very same condition if he doesn't also make the necessary lifestyle changes to deal with his diabetes and obesity.

Sometimes God's direct intervention is more obvious. Samantha may learn out of her own pain to receive God's forgiveness for some of the choices she has made and learn to forgive both herself and those who have wronged her. Her guilt and anxiety can be healed. Out of that relief her physical pain and her relationship with her husband may improve. Whether or not she becomes pregnant, she'll have experienced healing. She can walk into the future with hope and joy.

Can you see now why God's healing usually involves a process? There's a lot of work to be done. Your part in the process is to make every area of your life as open and available to Him as you can.

And then to do the next right thing.

Where does healing begin?
Wherever you're open to it.

Sometimes medical treatments may help the healing process to begin. Sometimes physical lifestyle changes will improve your well-being, give you hope, and lead to healing in other areas as well. Sometimes people around you provide the encouragement, comfort, and love that helps you care enough about yourself to make necessary changes, and healing begins. And sometimes God reaches into your life directly and heals a part of you no human being could ever have touched. And when you respond with gratitude and courage to live in the way He intends, that healing process just keeps on going.

True healing involves every part of you—your body, mind, and soul. And that's a beautiful thing.

Suggested Discussion Questions:

1. *What does "healing" mean to you? What would it look like for you to be healed?*

2. *Have you experienced healing in some area of your life? What was that like? In what area(s) do you need healing now?*

3. *What are some specific steps someone can take who desires to experience healing?*

Suggested Action Steps:

1. *On a piece of paper make two lists: the first of those wounds you have received from others and the second of those wounds you have helped inflict upon yourself.*
2. *Looking at your list of wounds, which do you think is the biggest foundational wound in your life?*
3. *Spend some time talking with God about any steps you can take to move toward healing in that area.*

Scripture to Contemplate or Memorize:

"Praise the LORD, O my soul, and forget not all his benefits—who forgives all your sins and heals all your diseases." (Psalm 103:2,3)

Chapter 12

What Does "Healthy" Look Like?

DRIVING THROUGH a major US city, I was scanning through the channels on the car radio. The host of a locally popular talk show was promoting healthy living, focusing on natural foods and supplements. She was a breast cancer survivor, and her passion to help others gain physical health seemed obvious.

Then she made a comment that shocked me: "I take over 60 pills a day, all of them supplements. I take no medications."

Now the idea of "natural" is a good one. I love "natural"! But 60 pills a day? There's absolutely no way even the most brilliant scientist/doctor/nutritionist can tell you what effect that amount and variety of substances may have on your body. This isn't about science. It isn't about "natural." This is about a desperation to be healthy.

I can sympathize with this talk show host: surviving cancer gives you a whole different perspective on life. When you've been seriously ill you'll do just about anything to regain your physical health.

And that goes for any area of life. When you've experienced depression, you may do just about anything to regain your mental/emotional ability to function. When you go through the wrenching pain of divorce, you may do almost anything to prevent a recurrence of that kind of pain. When you escape the bondage of addiction, you may take extraordinary steps to remain free in the future. When you feel the heaviness of legalism and guilt, you may run away from religion completely in your desperation to break free.

Think of the billions of dollars spent and the entire industries built around people trying to get healthy or feel better in some way. That includes weight loss systems, nutritional supplements, plastic surgery, life coaching, marital counseling, stress management and wellness seminars, retreats, and products, and in fact a large portion of the healthcare industry itself. It's only in the last several decades that much of this phenomenon has come to be. Come to think of it, what did people do before self-help groups, General Nutrition Centers, and bariatric surgery?

I'm being only slightly facetious. There's much of value in the various products, services, and industries trying to help people experience a better life. But what are we really after? What kind of "health" are we trying to achieve? If some magic potion could make you instantly "healthy," would you recognize yourself? Would you know it when you got there?

"If you aim at nothing," someone has quipped, "you are sure to reach it every time." While God never shows us every detail of the future He has for us, He allows enough sneak previews to make us hungry for it. He calls us to a life that's more challenging, meaningful, and abundant than anything we could ask for or achieve on our own.

As we close this first section, let's paint a picture of what healthy looks like. This is exactly what I believe Jesus meant when He said, "I have come that they may have life, and have it to the full" (John 10:10; "have it more abundantly" in the KJV).

And here's a hint: it won't take 60 pills a day to get there!

Fully Alive Physically

God cares about your body. He created it. It's His temple through His Holy Spirit (1 Corinthians 6:19). When He was here on Earth, Jesus spent much of His time healing people physically (Mathew 4:24; Luke 6:19). God wants you well!

That doesn't mean He isn't with you when you're sick, or that He guarantees a completely illness-free life in the here and now. We still live in a sinful, messed up world. But as your healthy lifestyle and

God's blessing work together, your physical body can be vibrantly alive (Romans 8:11).

That looks like:

- Generally strong and energetic a majority of the time

- Physically able to fully engage in the purpose God has for you

- No addictions or lifestyle illnesses

- Free from destructive lifestyle behaviors, such as substance abuse or unhealthy sexual behavior

Your physical body, and how you care for it, can be a demonstration of God's restoring, healing, and sustaining power.

Fully Alive Mentally and Emotionally

God cares about your mind and emotions. Rather than fear, He promised "power, . . . love, and . . . a sound mind" (2 Timothy 1:7, KJV). He goes about transforming and renewing your mind as you continue walking with Him (Romans 12:2; 1 Peter 1:13).

Many of the challenges you and I face in this world come through our thoughts and emotions. Remember that Jesus experienced fatigue, loneliness, and sadness (Mathew 26:37–40; Mark 4:38). We will continue to experience negative feelings as long as we're in this world, but we don't have to be controlled by them. You can have a sound mind and a healthy emotional life.

That looks like:

- Able to experience the full range of human emotions—sadness, grief, pain, joy, love, hope

- Not being stuck in a state of anger, fear, anxiety, bitterness, or other destructive emotions

- Mental and emotional ability to fulfill the purpose God has for you

- Mental clarity in discerning and interpreting God's voice

God promises you can have a mind like Jesus' (Philippians 2:5). That's not some nebulous spiritual idea; it's the result of His renewing of your mind.

Fully Alive Relationally

God cares about your relationships. God Himself is relational, and He desires relationship with you (Jeremiah 31:33,34). Families are a part of His plan (Psalm 68:6). The relationship between husband and wife is a picture of how close He wants to be with you and me (Ephesians 5:31,32), and our love for others is a demonstration of our connection with Him (John 13:35).

There is probably no bigger factor in your own well-being, or in the impact your life has on others, than the quality of your closest relationships. Those relationships can be characterized by the same quality of love and strength God demonstrates to us.

What that looks like:

- If you're married, your relationship with your spouse characterized by love and respect
- If you're single, living a full and vibrant life connected with others in healthy ways
- Living with sexual integrity, whether married OR single
- Having a full range of connections with others, characterized by mutuality, love, and growth

You're going to be living in relationship with other people for eternity. The richness of that life can begin now.

Fully Alive Spiritually

God cares about your heart, your innermost being, your soul, your spirit. That's the part of you that connects with God most directly. It's precious, and it's worth protecting with everything you have (Proverbs 4:23).

There's an all-out assault going on, a battle for your heart. As long as we live in this world, heart wounds and battle scars mean that we'll need God's presence to keep, preserve, and make alive this most unique and valuable part of who we are. Regardless of any other circumstances, God will strengthen our hearts (Ephesians 3:16–19).

What that looks like:

- A relationship with God that is resilient, growing, and real
- Continuing to experience God's transforming power in all aspects of your life
- Participating in the advance of God's kingdom on Earth
- Demonstrating hope for the future in the midst of troubles now

God's presence making your inner being fully alive will "leak out" and make the other parts of you alive as well.

Does that picture of "healthy" sound like an impossible dream? It isn't! It's never too late to get better, and it's never too early to start.

Rather than becoming discouraged by such an ambitious goal, let it inspire you, encourage you, and motivate you to work together with God more than ever before in finding and living the full life He has for you.

In the next section we'll focus on the aspect of life that probably makes the biggest difference in your daily sense of well-being—the quality of your relationships.

Suggested Discussion Questions:

1. *Read one or more of the Scripture references in this chapter. Is your life now demonstrating the aspect of health the verse portrays?*

2. *In which of these areas—physical, mental/emotional, relational, or spiritual—do you feel most in need of becoming more fully alive?*

3. *In which of these areas do you find it hardest to believe you can become fully alive?*

Suggested Action Steps:

1. *For the next week, each day read one or more of the Scriptures mentioned in this chapter. For context, read also the surrounding verses. Imagine the kind of life God is talking about in that passage.*

2. *Choose one or more of these verses that speak most to the kind of "fully alive" for which you're hungry. Write the verse(s) on a card, and place it where you will see it every day.*

3. *Write out your answer to this question: Of what would I have to let go to have this "fully alive" kind of life? This is definitely something to start thinking about.*

Scripture to Contemplate or Memorize:

"The thief comes only to steal and kill and destroy; I have come that they may have life, and have it to the full." (John 10:10)

Part Two

HEALTHY RELATIONSHIPS

"A new command I give you: Love one another. As I have loved you, so you must love one another. By this all men will know that you are my disciples, if you love one another." (JOHN 13:34,35)

"I have decided to stick with love. Hate is too great a burden to bear." (MARTIN LUTHER KING JR.)

Chapter 13

How Relationships Affect Your Health

IN A CLASSIC Peanuts cartoon Linus wants to be a doctor. The always negative Lucy says he can never be one because he doesn't love mankind. Linus retorts, "I love mankind . . . it's PEOPLE I can't stand!"[1]

Do you ever feel like Linus? Having good relationships with people may seem like a nice idea, but sometimes you just can't stand them.

Like them or lump them, you can't get away from people. Learning how to deal with them may be one of the most important things affecting the quality of your life. Specifically, the quality and quantity of your relationships does affect your physical and mental health. As social scientists have concluded, "Adults who are more socially connected are healthier and live longer than their more isolated peers."[2] Here are a few of the specific research findings this article summarizes:

- Children raised in supportive environments develop healthier immune, endocrine, and nervous systems that continue to impact their health as adults.

- Adolescents growing up in supportive environments

manifest significantly lower rates of substance abuse, mental health problems, and dangerous sexual practices.

- Adults with strong, positive social ties engage in healthier lifestyle practices, live longer, and develop fewer chronic diseases than those without them.
- Marital history over one's lifetime dramatically affects physical and mental health as one ages.
- Stressed or conflicted social relationships are costly to physical and mental health.

OK. We've commented on the research. Is any of that surprising? But what really matters is much more personal than any research. For you, the crux of the issue may sound much more like:

- Will my mother ever allow me to be an adult?
- What can I do instead of eating when I feel lonely?
- I can't stand one more day of work with such a demeaning boss.
- How can I keep from being depressed or desperate over still being single?
- My marriage is on life support, and I can't eat or sleep because of it.

We have a lot more control over the quality of our relationships than we may think. Our relationships change as we go through the stages of our lives, but at each stage we need people.

Here are a few questions to think about:

- What role do people play in your world?
- Do you see people and relationships as a net benefit or a net loss in your life?
- Which do you think is more significant, the impact other people have on you or the impact you have on other people?

- How do you deal with the truly difficult people in your life?
- Who can you not imagine living without?
- Whom would you prefer to have removed from your life?

Whether you're a social butterfly or hardly ever speak a word to another human being, your life involves people. There's your family of origin, your spouse or romantic partner (or lack thereof), and possibly children. There are friends (none, few, or many), church associations, coworkers, boss and/or employees, and many others. In some way you will have to interact with all of these different people. That's what this section of this book is about.

Attitudes about People

In all your relationships there are two bad attitudes about people that can make your interactions very difficult and unhealthy. Here they are.

1. **I'm entitled! Everyone owes me something.**
   "The bank owes me an easy way to borrow money. The government owes me a top education. The boss owes me a job. My friend owes me time and attention. My coworkers owe me a comfortable workplace. The pastor owes me a personal visit. If everybody around me doesn't fulfill their obligation to me, I'm miserable and angry. If something isn't right in my world, it's your fault!"

   Do you hear how that sounds? Yes, the other people and institutions in your life do have their responsibilities—to you and to others. Sometimes they meet those obligations well, and sometimes they don't.

   But the kind of mentality that's focused only on getting what you want and need is guaranteed to make you constantly upset. Thinking this way says, "I'm the center of the universe. Everybody must adjust to whatever is convenient for me." And that's bound, sooner or later, to conflict with reality.

2. **I don't matter to anybody. Nobody cares about me at all.**
   "Nobody knows or cares anything about the real me. The only way to make myself worth anything is to do exactly what you want and expect of me. I try and figure out what you think of me and then adjust my behavior to what I think you want. If you don't approve of me I'm not worth anything. If I try hard enough, maybe you'll be happy with me, and then I can be OK."

   That attitude will also leave you frustrated and usually alone. It takes a certain degree of maturity to realistically understand what you have to offer in this world and not to worry too much if others don't always agree with how you offer it. You may not be the most important person to every individual in your life, but you are important to some. There may be some people who don't agree with you or even like you, but there are others who will experience you as a hero.

On Whom Do You Focus?

Jesus loved everybody. But He didn't like everyone to the same degree. When He was on Earth Jesus spent the majority of His time with a comparatively small group of people, especially His twelve disciples. He interacted with difficult people only when He had a clear reason to do so. He spent most of his time and energy with people who:

1. Wanted what He had to offer and were willing to accept it (Luke 5:31; 16:12).

2. Could understand Him or give something of value to Him (Luke 8:3; John 11:5).

Relating to others in a healthy way includes deciding to spend most of your time and energy on relationships with people from whom you can learn and benefit or to whom you can give something.

- Some people tear you down: don't spend much time around them.

- You want to be more like some people: treasure opportunities to spend time with them, and study them.

- Some people enrich you and build you up just from being around them: be there as often as you can.

- Some people need—and more importantly, value—what you have to offer: give of yourself generously.

Viewing relationships in a healthy way means accepting people for who they are. Where you can truly help, offer that help freely. Don't try to change people who don't want to change. Reaching out in friendship means that you'll have friends. Seeing people in this way means that you can enjoy the richness they bring to life. That's healthy.

Much of the rest of this section will address marriage, but many of the ideas apply to all interpersonal relationships. When people come to the end of their lives, what usually matters most to them are the relationships they've had or didn't have. Make those relationships count now.

Suggested Discussion Questions:

1. *In what areas do you see an entitlement mentality in yourself or the people around you? Give some examples.*

2. *Where do you see an "I don't matter" mentality in yourself or in others around you? Give some examples.*

3. *Discuss how Jesus chose the people with whom He spent time and energy. How might you follow His example?*

Suggested Action Steps:

1. *Write down the names of the people you think about most often during an average day or week. They may be your parents, spouse or boyfriend, friends, coworkers, boss, children, students, employees, etc.*

2. *Look at your list. Are there some people on it who are tearing you down? How can you lessen the impact they have on your life?*

3. *What relationship do you need or want to work on strengthening? Do one thing this week to reach out to that person.*

Scripture to Contemplate or Memorize:

"For we are to God the aroma of Christ among those who are being saved and those who are perishing. To the one we are the smell of death; to the other, the fragrance of life. And who is equal to such a task?" (2 Corinthians 2:15,16)

Chapter 14

Family of Origin: No More Drama

AFTER HANGING UP the phone from talking with her mother, Larissa felt as though she could hardly breathe. Even though her mother was eighty years old and in a nursing home, she could still make Larissa feel as though she were seven years old and a bad little girl. The guilt, confusion, and anger she felt every time she spoke with her mother was exhausting. So, of course, she rarely visited.

"My mother doesn't like me, and she tells me so often," Larissa wrote to me. "It takes me a few days to regain my emotional stability after every visit. Am I being a bad person by not wanting to see my mother more often?"

You can't choose your parents. Or your brothers, sisters, and other family members. If your family of origin was reasonably healthy you probably don't think much about how you relate to them today. You look forward to family gatherings and keep in touch often.

There is invariably some tension as young people grow up and leave home, but healthy families celebrate such transitions. While still connected, you develop a life of your own, and you're at least somewhat proud of your parents and the legacy they've left you.

But not all families are so healthy. Some significant measure of dysfunction seems to be the norm in most families. Volumes have been written on the topic, and the mental health field has provided numerous careers devoted to helping those from unhealthy families learn to function better in the present.

Growing up in a home marked by alcohol, drugs, rage, criminal behavior, or violence leaves permanent scars on your soul. Perhaps you were on the receiving end of physical, verbal, or sexual abuse, or of neglect. Perhaps your parents split up, or you don't even know one or either of them. Perhaps poverty, excessive legalism, mental illness, or constant drama affected your home.

Where you come from affects you. How your parents handled conflict, their work ethic, family traditions, ideas about money and marriage and government and God—you unconsciously picked up their values and attitudes about all of those things and more. Even if you didn't like or feel close to one or both of your parents, their view of the world was your original one.

If your family of origin was less than healthy, you may naturally want to throw out their worldview. But it isn't that simple. The truth is, you learned by example. We repeat what we've experienced until and unless we face the reality of what our home was like and make the effort to learn new ways of living.

Simply saying "I'll never repeat that" doesn't work. Learning by experience has been just too powerful. But you can consciously choose and develop new behaviors to replace those you don't want to repeat.

Most people who grew up in a dysfunctional home will one day have to face the matter of forgiveness. Forgiving your parents may be one of the hardest steps you'll have to take in growing up. You have a choice about how long you allow that abuse or dysfunction to control your life. Choosing to let it go is the only way to finally become free of any negative baggage. We'll talk more about forgiveness in chapter 29.

A Healthy Relationship with Your Family

If you came from a great family, be grateful. The values, attitudes, skills, and relationships you gained form a wonderful foundation for building your own life. Use them as an opportunity to get a jump-start on maturity. You can leverage those strengths even more. You can stand on their shoulders, so to speak, and extend the reach of your own life even farther. You honor them best by not resting on the past but by taking what you've received and using it in your own life to make a positive difference for others.

If your family of origin wasn't so great, you have extra challenges, but you also have some unexpected opportunities. You can use the negatives as encouragement to develop better character qualities, such as compassion, perseverance, and courage. You may have to work hard to evaluate and change your values, attitudes, skills, and relationships. And you may need some help to do so. You can still honor your family by accepting any of the good aspects they passed along, refusing to continue the negative behaviors, and deliberately moving forward.

You will know you've reached real healing and maturity regarding your family of origin when you can:

- Look honestly at the truth about them without becoming angry, resentful, or ashamed.
- Honor and respect them for the positive things they gave you, even if most of their legacy was painful.
- Stay connected without being controlled or manipulated.
- Value your roots without defining yourself by them.
- Learn to take what's good and leave behind the rest.

You love your family members for who they are today and forgive them for the past, while still protecting yourself, if necessary, from further pain. You've felt the sting, looked reality in the face, and moved on.

No More Drama

Dysfunctional family life often includes a lot of drama. Your parents, especially, know how to push your buttons because they installed them!

Here are a few facts and tools to help you steer clear of the drama:

1. **You are only responsible for your own happiness.** That goes both ways: nobody else can make you happy or unhappy, and you aren't responsible for anyone else's happiness. While we do have an impact on one another, our mental and emotional state is our own responsibility. And their happiness is their responsibility alone.

2. **You can't change anyone else.** Knowing that a certain person is likely to act a certain way allows you to choose ahead of time whether, and how, to respond. You gain nothing by pretending they're healthy if they aren't, or wasting your energy trying to make them act differently.

3. **Your own attitude may be infectious.** If you're calm and pleasant, your demeanor may rub off on others. If you're upset, hurt, and angry, others will likely respond with a similar attitude. Taking charge of your own attitude is the only leverage you have, but sometimes it's enough.

4. **Learning emotional skills takes time.** Dealing with difficult people, or those who stir up drama, isn't a job for the faint of heart. And it's hardest if the difficult people are your parents. If you're struggling to know how to deal with the drama, give yourself some grace: it's isn't easy!

5. **It's OK to say NO.** You're not necessarily being selfish or difficult; sometimes saying NO is the only wise thing to do. And remember, "NO" is a complete sentence.

You can refuse to play your part in the ongoing production of "As the Family Turns." Just opt out!

It took Larissa a long time to realize that her mother's opinion of her didn't equate to the truth. God's opinion of her was much more important. She also learned to have another friend or family member with her when she visited her mother. Sometimes she would let her mother's calls go to voicemail and respond to them when she felt able. She would show her mother love when she visited, and she became better at not bringing her mother's negativity home with her.

We all come from a family. Every family has some good aspects and some not so positive. Growing past the drama takes time and grace, but you can do it.

Suggested Discussion Questions:

1. *Describe some of the ways by which you've observed your parents (or others who affected your early life) handling stress or conflict. How did that affect the way you learned to handle stress or conflict?*

2. *What are some healthy ways of relating to a difficult parent? Describe a particular circumstance and suggest what a good response might be.*

3. *What did you observe your parents doing that you determined never to do yourself? Have you learned any alternative ways of behaving?*

Suggested Action Steps:

1. *Write a letter to one or both of your parents, thanking them for the positive things they've passed on to you. Don't include anything negative. If they're still alive, consider reading or sending it to them.*

2. *Think of your last difficult encounter with your parent(s) or another family member. What can you do differently next time? Write down your ideas to help you prepare.*

3. *Spend at least 15 minutes talking to God about areas in which you need Him to be the parent you needed but never had.*

Scripture to Contemplate or Memorize:

"A father to the fatherless, a defender of widows, is God in his holy dwelling." (Psalm 68:5)

Note: If the concept of God as Father is difficult or painful for you because you experienced abuse, neglect, or other serious pain from a parent, be patient with yourself. This book isn't a place to fully explore the impact of childhood abuse, but please know that God is patient with you also. Find a Christian counselor with whom you feel safe and get some help.

Chapter 15

When You're Single

RHONDA WAS BECOMING desperate. She was inching closer to 40 and was still single. She felt her biological clock ticking, but that wasn't the worst part. She was lonely! Why couldn't she find a good husband? What was she doing wrong? The guys at church were neither interested nor interesting. Should she join Christian Mingle? Was it too late?

Linda had become a widow six years earlier, at the age of 42. Raising two teenagers alone was hard. She had just ended a one-year relationship with a man she had hoped to marry, but the longer they were together the more convinced she became that this wasn't the man God wanted for her. But now she was so lonely. Were there any "good" men left?

Whether you're never married or single again after divorce or death, living alone gets old. I know: I was single until I got married at 48 years old. I remember seeing all the married couples in church and feeling as though I wasn't quite part of the inside crowd because I was single. I used to wonder whether there was something wrong with me because no man wanted me.

Maybe you're single because you saw or experienced pain in the marriages you knew (such as that of your parents) and haven't wanted to even consider the idea. Maybe you're single because you got sexually involved in multiple relationships in the past and struggle now with guilt and wondering whether anyone would really want you. Maybe you're single because you got out of a bad marriage, and now you're saddled with all the baggage—both good (yes, that's quite possible) and bad.

Or maybe you're single just because—you're single.

And why does everyone keep asking your relationship status anyway? Isn't it enough to be JUST YOU?!

Whether or not you're happy about it, the single life does have some challenges.

First, what NOT to do. Being lonely can make you vulnerable. And that can get you into trouble. So please DON'T:

1. Grab onto the first available guy, regardless of whether or not he's good marriage material.

2. Ignore "red flags" in a potential spouse, believing that marriage will fix whatever is wrong.

3. Manipulate someone to "force" him into marrying you.

4. Lower your standards for what kind of spouse you'll accept.

5. Compromise your own integrity, feeling that's the only way to catch a potential husband.

A bad marriage is so much worse than being single. If you don't believe that, take a poll of your married friends. There are plenty of unhappily married people who would be glad to switch problems with you!

But knowing that doesn't ease the loneliness you feel or answer the Why? questions. So, what to do?

How to Be Happy Single
(and Prepare for Marriage If You Desire)

Learning to be happy in whatever state you find yourself (Philippians 4:11) is an important lesson. It's one I found difficult to master and didn't learn it until I was well into my forties. But it IS something you can learn. That doesn't mean that everything in your life is or will be perfect, or that you'll never feel lonely. But you really, truly can be happy.

Here are some skills you can learn that are guaranteed to bring you an honest measure of happiness:

1. **Choose to be happy.** This is the most important. By far the biggest determinant of your emotional state is your own decision. No other person or circumstance has enough power over you to MAKE you feel anything—unless you give them that power. You can choose to be happy, sad, miserable, lonely, angry, grateful, peaceful, or any other combination of emotions and attitudes.

2. **Learn to both give and receive.** Jesus said, "It is more blessed to give than to receive" (quoted by Paul in Acts 20:35). That isn't a cliché; it's true. Your own happiness will often be in direct proportion to how much you give to others. And along the way, learn to be grateful for the things that are given back to you.

3. **Become the right person.** Many single people focus on looking for the right person to marry. But if you want to marry a prince, you need to become a princess. Consciously focus on developing characteristics you want to have, such as integrity, joy, kindness, flexibility, courage, humor, and love. That will make you happier whatever your future relationship status may be, and you'll have more to offer if Mr. Right does come along.

4. **Keep your soul well fed.** No other human being can meet every inner need you have. YOU are responsible to find ways to stay filled up: same-sex friends or couples, artistic activities, rest, intellectual stimulation, time with God. Should you get married, your spouse may join you in many of those activities. But growing up means learning to feed yourself, whether or not you're single.

5. **Learn to know God as your Source.** Ultimately, good things such as security, guidance, protection, wisdom, love, and everything else that's important don't come primarily from parents, bosses, preachers, friends, or a husband. They ultimately come from God. When you can learn to experience God as your husband (Isaiah 54:5), the rest of the single life becomes easier.

You will only be happy married if you can learn to be happy single.

What about Sex?

Now a word about the really big question: What do I do about my sexuality if I'm single?

Here's the blunt truth:

- God invented sex, and He created man and woman to be sexual beings.

- God created sex to be ravishingly enjoyed by one man and one woman in marriage.

- Our sex-saturated culture has made it more difficult to embrace and maintain sexual integrity—whether we're married or single.

- God knows all of these realities. And He'll provide the grace you need to honor Him with your sexuality.

Without apology, I believe the biblical message is that the only legitimate place for sexual intimacy is between a man and a woman within the bounds of marriage. Sexual intimacy in any other context is wrong. I believe that's the only legitimate understanding of Scripture.

You may try to argue with me theologically, but what I believe you're really asking is "How can God expect me to remain single and not be sexually active?"

I know all about the physical and emotional urges, the cultural conditioning, the hormones, the biological clock, and the loneliness. I lived with all of that for 48 years. And as an OB/GYN physician and a Christian minister I see other women struggling with it every day.

So I'm going to suggest several steps that will help you maintain your sexual integrity, especially if you're single.

1. **Stay physically healthy.** You can hear God's voice more clearly and make wiser decisions with a healthy body and a clear mind.

2. **Guard your heart.** Don't give it away cheap. If you do, the hole in your heart will only be torn wider and deeper. It isn't worth it.

3. **Choose your mental diet carefully.** Your friends, your media choices, what you allow your mind to think about—make sure they support your sexual integrity. If they don't, just say no.

4. **Stay connected.** Find other healthy Christian adults to spend time with (same-sex friends or couples). Also seek out people in need whom you can help.

5. **Give God a chance.** Talk to Him about all your needs, sexual needs included. Ask all the Why? questions. Wrestle with the unfairness of it all. And give Him a chance to become Enough for you.

Being single isn't simply a prelude to being married. For my friends who are single, I want you to know that *you are* enough.

God sees and cares about you. And so do I.

Suggested Discussion Questions:

1. *What are some benefits of being single (i.e., spending your money as you wish)?*

2. *Isaiah 54:5 says, "For your Maker is your husband—the Lord Almighty is his name." Talk about what that means for you. How can God be like a husband to you?*

3. *What does "sexual integrity" mean to you? What does this look like for a single person?*

Suggested Action Steps:

1. *If you're single, write down some benefits of your status. Put that list where you can see it when you feel unhappy about your singleness.*

2. *Write down a list of things you would want from a husband. Take that list to God in prayer, and find out in how many of those ways God can become a Husband to you.*

3. *Take an honest inventory of your sexuality. Do you sense God asking you to change anything in that area? (You'll find more opportunities to address this in coming chapters.)*

Scripture to Contemplate or Memorize:

"For your Maker is your husband—the Lord Almighty is his name—the Holy One of Israel is your Redeemer; he is called the God of all the earth." (Isaiah 54:5)

Chapter 16

Red, Yellow, Green: Your Relationship Traffic Light

DID YOU EVER play the game "Red Light, Green Light" as a child? I did. One of us would be "It," and the others would line up at the starting line. When "It" would call out "Green Light," we'd each walk as fast as we could. But don't you dare take even one step after "It" called out "Red Light"! That meant you had to go back to the starting line and try again. The first one to reach the finish line without moving on red was rewarded with being the next "It."

The game sounded simple. And it was. But have you ever tried stopping instantly when you were trying to move as quickly as possible? It was a lot harder than you might think.

I doubt elementary students play "Red Light, Green Light" during recess any longer. With sophisticated playground equipment and sports programs in place, children now have much more entertaining things to do.

But we adults are very good at playing "Red Light, Green Light," not on the playground but in our relationships. And the stakes are so much higher than they were in childhood.

Your Relationship Traffic Light indicates how open, or closed, you are to a possible intimate relationship. It isn't that hard to tell the color of someone else's light, often without their even saying a word. You can tell by the way they carry themselves, by the way they look at someone else, by the way they dress, and by the smallest things they say or don't say.

You certainly know people who are calling out "Red Light." It's clear that they aren't open for business. Intimacy business, that is. Perhaps their heart is "taken." It may be that there's no place for you, or anyone else, to enter because their spouse or sweetheart has their whole heart. Or perhaps they're so focused on work or career that they have nothing left for intimacy. Or maybe they demonstrate such emotional brokenness that an intimate advance would just not happen. Who do you know who clearly signals a red light?

Then there's the Yellow Light. Yellow means Caution, right? Nobody would call someone with a yellow light flirtatious. But their light isn't red either. You could imagine that if just the right situation presented itself, well, who knows what might happen? Perhaps they're needy or would truly welcome a relationship but just aren't advertising the fact openly at this point. Perhaps their current relationship is unsatisfying and they're giving subtle clues that they're open to considering other options. You surely know someone who displays a yellow light.

And then there are those calling out "Green Light." Even if the door is closed, there's clearly no lock on it. By a laugh, a glance, a lingering touch, a phrase or a word, the way they dress, where they hang out, the message is clear. Their heart is open, available, waiting or asking for someone to enter. It wouldn't take much to initiate intimacy. Who around you is reflecting a green light?

What Color is Your Relationship Traffic Light?

The more important question is Which color relationship traffic light are YOU signaling? With the people with whom you interact at work, friends you meet socially, others at church, even on-line relationships, what color is your light? And remember, the color of your light is probably obvious to others without your ever saying a word.

Are you reflecting a red light? If you're married, or preparing to be married, can others tell that you're definitely closed for outside business? That intimate advances are clearly unwelcome? Even if you might appear a little stuffy and reserved, you're showing to everyone around you that your heart is taken and there's no place for anyone else.

Or perhaps you're showing a yellow light. No, the door isn't wide open, but it might not be tightly locked either. Maybe, just maybe, a little intimacy would be accepted. OK, nothing physical, at least not right now. But there's a little open crack in your heart, and if just the right key were found, perhaps someone might find entry.

Or is your light green? Your words might not say so, but your actions may indicate that your heart is available. You're searching, hungry, even fishing for the right response in someone else, indicating that intimacy would be welcome. And if a few choice personal words open the door further, Who knows? you might welcome a little more.

We can easily deceive ourselves into thinking that a "green light" is OK and that we can stop the process any time we want. Or at least a yellow light, right? "I'm being cautious: nothing will happen. I'm just having a little fun and being nice. I'm supposed to treat other people nicely, right?"

A traffic light is designed to do one thing only: stop cross-traffic so nobody gets hurt. If you run a red light, you might make it through the intersection without injury, but do you really want to risk the collision that may come if the cross-traffic is going too fast? In the childhood game, remember how hard it was to stop moving instantly when "It" shouted "Red Light"?

Years ago, before I knew my husband, I became acquainted with someone who was clearly flashing a green light. This was in a professional setting far away from where I lived. He was married, with children, and I was very single. Our professional activities afforded occasional opportunities for contact.

On one of these occasions I got a "green light" invitation from my professional friend. And I'm sorry to admit that I didn't immediately flash a red light in response. Thankfully, I did put on the brakes fast enough to prevent any actions I would later have had to regret. And I'm grateful that my relationship with God gave me the strength to do so while I still could.

That experience showed me that my light had undoubtedly been yellow on that occasion. While his "green light" invitation was his problem, I was responsible for ensuring that the only thing I displayed to a married man was a red light. And I'm very certain that, now that I'm married, my husband is the only person who sees my green light.

The color of your Relationship Traffic Light needs to be decided in advance. And your light's color is a natural result of everything else going on in your own heart. If you're getting responses from other people that aren't what you want or expect, check the color of your light. What kind of responses do you *really* wish to receive? How others respond may not be your problem. But at least you can make sure the messages you're sending are ones you won't later come to regret.

The heart is a vulnerable thing, very precious and even fragile. Something that valuable and susceptible needs to be guarded carefully. I pray that you'll value your heart as much as it's truly worth!

Suggested Discussion Questions:

1. *How can you tell the color of someone else's Relationship Traffic Light? What is there about what they do or say that lets you know?*

2. *How can you tell the color of your own Relationship Traffic Light?*

3. *How would someone go about changing the color of their Relationship Traffic Light?*

Suggested Action Steps:

1. *What color is your Relationship Traffic Light? How do you know? Write down your answer.*

2. *If you aren't sure about the answer to the previous question, find a safe friend or professional to give you feedback on what color light you are signaling.*

3. *Spend some time in prayer this week, asking God's opinion of your Relationship Traffic Light. Do you need to make any changes?*

Scripture to Contemplate or Memorize:

"Above all else, guard your heart, for it is the wellspring of life." (Proverbs 4:23)

Chapter 17

Why Is Sex So Slippery?

DIANE AND GWEN both jump from one intense, intimate relationship to another with barely a breath in between. Diane tends to marry her boyfriends; she believes that makes her relationships more legitimate. She's now preparing to marry husband number five. Gwen would rather not marry. "What's the point?" she asks. "It isn't going to last anyway." Neither Diane nor Gwen has ever been in a relationship that lasted more than five years, and they can't imagine life any other way.

At least one of our recent radio guests believes that marital infidelity is even more prevalent INSIDE the church than outside. Another of our radio professional friends just discovered that his wife was sleeping with another man. As a physician, I see women almost every week who are suffering the consequences of past or present sexually transmitted infections.

And we're just getting started.

Most preachers don't like to talk about this issue. Parents struggle to talk about it with their children. More public figures, both within and outside the church, have been scandalized by this than by probably any other sin. The world's "oldest profession" makes merchandise of what was intended to be sacred. Divorce and infidelity devastate the souls of men and women as little else can. Why?

Yes, we're talking about sex. And about how something God meant to be beautiful has so often become tangled up with pain, trauma, and dirt. So many of our troubles and hang-ups are in some way related to sex.

Why does pornography have such a hold on so many, both men and woman?[1] Why is casual sex such a trap for young people (and sometimes older people as well!)? Why does it sell so well—anything from cars to cleaning products, medications, and romance novels? Why the viciously strong feelings about same-sex relationships—by both those for and against? Why is the victimization of women and children (and even men) so often sexual in nature?

Something is going on here. You might say "That's just sin." And in the ultimate sense you're right. But why are we so vulnerable? Why can we get hurt so easily in this area? Why does it seem the enemy of our souls can so easily wreak havoc among us using these themes? And it's been that way ever since the days of Sarah, Tamar, Bathsheba, Rahab, and Gomer (Genesis 16:2–4; 38:13–18; Joshua 2:1; 2 Samuel 11:2–5; Hosea 1:2,3; 3:1–3).

Enough of the ugly descriptions of the state of our human relationships. And I'm not even talking right now about whose fault it all is. (Nor is this to undermine the many beautiful relationships that do exist.) I believe there is a wonderful and almost scandalous truth in the midst of this mess that makes it all make sense.

Attempting an Answer

There's really only one way to answer the Why? And it has to do with the very way we are created:

God made us for Himself.

That's both the wonderful and the scandalous truth. Our whole being—body, mind, and soul—is made in His image. We can't separate our physical desires from our spiritual longings because in reality they're one and the same. We need, we crave the intimacy and connection— physically, emotionally, and spiritually—for which we were fashioned.

Simply trying to deny one's desires won't work, and it puts us in a very vulnerable place. I believe the reason intimacy and sexual stuff get us into trouble so often is that they touch the very core of our nature. And that's the reason sex can be either so spectacular or so devastating. (Remember, sexuality and intimacy are related, but they're by no means the same.)

When a man stranded on the ocean drinks salt water in an attempt to satisfy his thirst it only makes his cravings worse. Our desires in and of themselves are right. God built them into our beings. Yet in our sinful world the object(s) of our desires may be unhealthy, dangerous, or distorted. But our longings, our cravings, our desires are as much a part of who we are as human beings as are our hands and feet. And God engineered us that way.

God created us that way for a reason. He wants us to long for and need relationship. Close, intimate, personal interconnectedness. It's the only way we can be who He created us to be.

The Fulfilling of Desire

Do you believe for one moment that God is surprised by the pain sexually related stuff has caused in our world? He obviously knew the risk, and He judged that creating us as sexual beings was worth that risk. He knew that building into us the need for close, personal, intimate (physical and spiritual) relationships would leave us vulnerable.

But He also knew that without that need, and the pressing desire to fulfill it, we would never reach our highest joy, either in this world or in eternity.

And without that longing we would never connect with Him at the level HE desired.

St. Augustine prayed, "Lord, give me chastity . . . but not just yet!" He knew firsthand the struggles our desires can cause. But he went on to say, "Thou hast made us for thyself, O Lord, and our heart is restless until it finds its rest in Thee."[2]

So what do we do with our desire? Even sexual desire? I offer these thoughts:

1. **Embrace desire.** God built it into you. Physical, emotional, and spiritual desires are God-given, and they can't be completely separated. Embracing desire

doesn't mean, however, automatically doing whatever you want. There are consequences.

2. **Guard your heart** (Proverbs 4:23). As beautiful as desire can be, it can also be deadly. Realize that the object of your desire may not be that which will fulfill your true longing. Watch over your heart with great care. Choose consciously and carefully where and to whom to open your heart.

3. **Know where you're vulnerable.** What's OK for me may not be OK for you, and vice versa. The question isn't "Can I get away with it?" but "Will this make me vulnerable?" Please don't take a chance!

4. **Ask God to fill your love cup.** Give Him time and opportunity to meet the deepest needs in your soul. After He fills you up, you won't be as likely to crave salt water when you're thirsty.

5. **Freely give.** When you help fill another's love cup, your own will be filled to overflowing. Love your spouse ravishingly. Hug your kids. Hug a friend, or someone else in need. Love them not for what they can give you back but for no other reason than to love.

If you're reading this, you've probably been hurt somehow in the realm of intimate personal relationships. Who hasn't been hurt here? Perhaps you've followed your heart's desires to unhealthy or dangerous ends. Perhaps you feel grief, shame, guilt, or loss because of your desires and how they've been filled—or not fulfilled.

But there's good news! It's never too late. God's love can fill you up and wash you clean, no matter where you've been. Let Him fulfill your deepest desires. He wants to. He made you for Himself, and no one here on Earth will ever cherish and love you as He does.

Suggested Discussion Questions:

1. *What's the "craziest" thing you've done out of a desire for intimacy? How did it turn out?*

2. *How do you feel about the idea that God made our physical, emotional, and spiritual desires to be interconnected? Does that sound like good news or bad news?*

3. *What would it look like for you to have God "fill your love cup"? If that sounds foreign to you, listen to others talk about what it means to them.*

Suggested Action Steps:

1. *In what area(s) have you been hurt in the realm of intimate personal relationships? (Ouch!) Write a story or poem about your experience.*

2. *Is there some way in which you've been hurt in intimacy that you've never grieved? Find a time to have a good cry over it.*

3. *Find a quiet place to pray. Ask God to come and intimately touch your heart. Spend at least 15 minutes listening. See whether God shows up.*

Scripture to Contemplate or Memorize:

"As the deer pants for streams of water, so my soul pants for you, O God." (Psalm 42:1)

Chapter 18

The Benefits of Healthy Sex Beyond the Bedroom

TRY THIS LITTLE experiment the next time you're standing in line or waiting at the doctor's office. I warn you: you'll need to keep the mental pictures in this experiment to yourself. This is, as it were, "for *your* mind only!"

Here's the experiment: look at the women you see. Even, or especially, the ones you don't know. Really look at them. Now imagine what kind of sex life they have. Don't ask them, of course. But from the way they carry themselves and how they relate to other people you can probably get a pretty good idea.

You might see:

- The harried housewife whose husband has lost interest in her
- The young woman living with her boyfriend and hoping not to get pregnant
- The survivor of childhood abuse who still suffers from PTSD
- The stale and bitter senior living alone, and lonely

- The angry divorcee now busy trying to make her own life

- The happy grandmother still in love with the same man after decades of marriage

Perhaps some of your imaginings would turn out to be wrong. But doesn't that experiment open your eyes to how a woman's sex life often spills over into the other areas of her life?

By now you know my position: I believe sex was created by God as something wonderful, to be relished and ravishingly enjoyed between one man and one woman within marriage. That's it. Any other use of sex is wrong and gets us into trouble. You may not agree with me, but I believe that's the way God intended things to be.

Sex touches something very deep within us. There's probably no other area, short of our understanding of God's love, that so strongly impacts our sense of identity and value as sexuality does. The correlation is strong:

- If you've been violated sexually (as a child or as an adult), you probably feel dirty, vulnerable, and ashamed. Taking a bath doesn't make you feel clean; the violation goes much deeper. Through taking advantage of your body, your soul has been assaulted.

- If you struggle with maintaining sexual integrity, it's likely you feel guilty, ashamed, and hopeless. Other sinful acts or addictions may also be hard to conquer, but sexual issues go even deeper. You may feel profoundly isolated from God and from others.

- If your sexual relationship with your spouse is full of conflict, control, manipulation, or refusal, you probably feel frustrated, angry, isolated, and powerless. You may tolerate each other, but you don't feel connected or secure.

- If you enjoy a healthy, interesting, and mutually satisfying sexual relationship with your husband, you likely feel loved, cherished, fulfilled, and confident. The comfort, exhilaration, intimacy, and safety of healthy sex within marriage impact you far beyond the bedroom.

If you don't like what sex and sexuality mean in your life right now, let me encourage you not to ignore the issue. Think of your sexuality as a picture of the state of your inner soul. Perhaps it isn't the only or the most complete picture, but it's at least one very revealing picture.

What Good Sex Means

Assume for a moment that a strong and mutual sexual relationship with your husband is possible. What feelings would that stimulate in you? How would it make you feel outside the bedroom?

Here are some components of healthy marital sex:

- Mutually satisfying
- Exciting, interesting
- Bonding (yes, oxytocin really does create feelings of closeness![1])
- Vulnerable, yet safe
- Comforting
- Intimate (emotionally and spiritually, as well as physically)
- Being wanted
- Being known
- Being cherished
- Confident as a woman

Sex doesn't automatically bring on those good feelings. And while it's possible to experience those feelings without sex, good marital sex without doubt brings them on. Not every one of them every time. But doesn't that list make you wish you could have more of whatever would make you feel that way?

That's also one big reason why sex outside of marriage is problematic. When you offer physical intimacy without the commitment and covenant of marriage, many of those other benefits can't completely happen. You may think you can experience bonding, safe vulnerability, and being known, but outside of marriage that's all superficial.

Even at its best, sex in marriage isn't the answer to everything. Only God can meet every one of our needs. In fact, every one of those characteristics of good marital sex listed above can also be a characteristic of our relationship with God.

How Do You Get There?

So how do you approach that impossible dream?

Here are a few things you can do if intimacy with your husband isn't resulting in those other benefits:

1. **Get a medical evaluation.** Physical pain during sex is a serious mood killer for women. There are also some hormonal problems and a few medications that can decrease a woman's sexual response. Your gynecologist is a good place to start.

2. **Face your sexual past.** If you're dealing with anxiety, shame, or guilt over something in your past, face the issue head-on. Did you have unwanted sexual experiences as a child, or as an adult? Are you troubled by infidelity, a previous abortion, or an STD? Get some help if you need to. Don't ignore the issue.

3. **Take care of yourself.** Physically, emotionally, and spiritually. Sexual intimacy is meant to be a mutually giving experience. If your cup is empty, you won't have much to give. Take responsibility for doing what you need to do in order to stay filled up.

4. **Nurture the emotional climate in your marriage.** A woman has a much harder time than a man does in brushing aside unfinished business and enjoying sex. Invest in learning how to communicate, forgive, be a friend, and connect with your husband in other ways also.

5. **Talk about sex.** That's right! Talk about sex with your husband. At a time when neither of you is feeling sexual, bring up the subject. Ask questions such as What's good about the intimacy between us? What isn't working? What do you want? How can we make intimacy better for both of us?

6. **Make the mental leap.** For women especially, a huge part of sex happens in the mind. In many cases you can CHOOSE to respond sexually. That doesn't mean giving in to sex when you'll end up resenting it later. But it does mean choosing to respond when you can. And your body will often follow along by responding.

7. **Pray about it.** God created sex, and He's interested in helping you maximize this important aspect of your marriage. Perhaps you need to seek Him for some inner healing. He is certainly the best One to fill your soul and give you wisdom in this and every other area of your marriage.

Healthy sexual intimacy in marriage goes beyond the physical satisfaction. It has an effect on your life in many other ways. And best of all, it's a demonstration of the intimacy God desires with each of us.

It's worth working on.

Suggested Discussion Questions:

1. How does the quality of a woman's sex life show up in the other areas of her relationships? Other areas of her life?

2. Name several aspects of great marital sex that are important to you.

3. What do you think are the biggest roadblocks to a better sex life between you and your husband?

Suggested Action Steps:

1. *Are there any sexual hang-ups with which you struggle? If you haven't dealt with them, write down two things*

you are going to do about the problem (e.g., join an online community for support, talk with a pastor, or see a Christian counselor).

2. Make an appointment to talk with your husband about sex. Write down some specific questions for each of you to ask the other.

3. Read the Song of Songs (Song of Solomon). Notice the rich sexual imagery, and see how it impacts your view of sex.

Scripture to Contemplate or Memorize:

"My lover is mine and I am his; he browses among the lilies." (Song of Songs 2:16)

"I belong to my lover, and his desire is for me." (Song of Songs 7:10)

Chapter 19

Contraception, STDs, and Other Complications

I SAW SUZANNE in the office just a few days ago. She was in tears over her boyfriend's behavior and what she called "my own stupidity." She had discovered that he was having sex with another woman while professing to still be with her. Now, two months after their relationship had ended, she was coming in to be tested for sexually transmitted diseases, while still scared about the possibility of pregnancy.

Corrine called our radio program recently. Years earlier she had been lured into a relationship by a man on the internet who claimed to be a sincere Christian. A quick and intense relationship had led to sex, then marriage, and finally a messy divorce. Today she is still living with shame over her unwise actions and wonders whether God will ever bring her a godly husband.

Sonya wasn't my regular patient, but she sought me out and asked me for a prescription for Valtrex (used to decrease the recurrence of genital herpes). She tearfully told me about running away from home at 18, living with an older man for a few months, and then returning home with shame—and herpes. Now as a wife, mother of three girls, and Christian bookstore owner she drives miles out of her way to fill her prescription at a pharmacy where no one she knows will see her.

Naomi wrote to me recently. She's in her fifties, single, assistant to the pastor at her church, and full of regrets. She badly wanted to be a wife and mother and entered into a sexual relationship with a fellow church member who was also a drug addict, hoping he would become her husband and that she could fix him in the process. Many months and many tears later he is gone, and she is left with only guilt.

These are just a few of the stories I carry in my heart. I know these women personally. These aren't made-up stories. And I could share many more.

The message: condoms, birth control pills, and Gardasil do NOT make for safe sex!

There's no condom that will prevent a broken heart.

There's no shot that will vaccinate against shame and guilt.

Every day I work in the office or take a shift at the hospital I treat women for the physical consequences of sexual activity. But what prescription can I write to cure a broken heart or a crushed soul?

I know some of the reasons we women get into such difficulties. We're lonely, we want to be connected to someone, and we choose to believe the best about this guy. "THIS TIME it will be different," we assure ourselves. Emotions, hormones, and our human-ness scream louder than our sane thoughts, leaving us only to be disappointed later.

The Medical Side

I wear two hats when it comes to women's health: Medical Doctor and Doctor of Ministry. That's really why you're reading this book. I'm going to put on my Medical Doctor hat here for just a moment. There are plenty of other places you can go to get medical information on which contraception method is most effective and what kinds of symptoms may indicate a sexually transmitted infection.

There are two things I know for sure. First, the only way to completely prevent pregnancy is to not have sex, or to have a hysterectomy. I can't tell you the number of women I've seen who became pregnant while using some form of birth control. (Of course, I've seen many, many more women become pregnant while not using birth control at all!)

And, second, the only way to completely prevent STDs is to not have sex, or to remain in a mutually monogamous relationship. And I'm not talking about "serial monogamy": when you have sex with someone, you are also having sex with everyone they have ever had sex with. And I can't tell you how many women I've seen who've contracted an STD when they thought they were "being careful."

The Heart Problems

Now my Medical Doctor hat comes off, in a sense. The questions you're probably asking have more to do with how to take these medical, personal, emotional, and sexual issues and live with them in a spiritually realistic and responsible way. Here are a few of my answers.

> Q. Can God agree with me using contraception?
> A. In the Bible, sex isn't only about having children. There's enough in Scripture about how God celebrates the fulfilling and bonding aspects of sex between husband and wife that I believe He can clearly bless a couple who chooses to use contraception (see Song of Songs; Hebrews 13:4). Pregnancy is always possible, but choosing if or when to have children can be a separate decision from when to be sexually active in marriage. And God smiles on a couple who chooses to celebrate their bond for reasons other than procreation.
>
> Q. What if I've been sexually active when I shouldn't have been in the past. Can God forgive me?
> A. Yes! A thousand times yes! He is faithful to forgive whenever we ask (1 John 1:9). The reason many find it difficult to accept God's forgiveness and even to forgive themselves when it comes to sexual sins is related to how deep the issue goes in one's soul. Paul said that "he who sins sexually sins against his own

body" (1 Corinthians 6:18). The reality is also that the emotional and physical consequences of that sexual activity may take time to heal. But God can and does bring healing even when we do foolish things and experience the painful consequences. That's so important, and so true.

Q. Are you saying I shouldn't be sexually active if I'm not married? That isn't realistic!

A. First of all, it isn't me who's saying that. God is. And yes, it IS possible. I know what it's like to live single: I did so for 48 years. Go back and read the last section of chapter 15. There I offer some specific ideas on how to maintain sexual integrity when you aren't married.

Q. I'm married, and I have an STD. What am I supposed to do?

A. If you brought the STD into your marriage, you need to be honest with your husband. If you know it wasn't you, the situation becomes more challenging. Some STDs (such as HPV, herpes, or even chlamydia) can remain hidden for quite some time: I've seen many women for whom the most likely source of an STD was their husband's sexual activity before marriage. A number of STDs may cause no symptoms in a man who carries it for quite some time and then exposes his wife. That's why it's a good idea for both partners to be tested for STDs prior to marriage if either has previously been sexually active. Of course there's also the possibility that your husband has had a sexual contact outside the marriage. If you suspect that to be the case, the time is right for prayer; counsel; and slow, careful thinking.

How many times I've wanted to say to the women I meet or treat as a doctor, "Just don't do it! ANY sex before or outside marriage is too risky! Please don't throw everything away for a momentary pleasure, or for a man's lies!"

But what I DO say, whenever I can, is this: "Today can be the first day of the rest of your life. You don't have to give away your heart or your body. God made you for more than this. He's got a great future for you!"

If just one woman, young or old, reads this and stops to consider saying NO to sex before or outside of marriage, I'll be grateful.

And if just one woman, young or old, reads this and finds hope to experience God's forgiveness for her sexual past and its consequences, it will have been worth it.

Suggested Discussion Questions:

1. *If you could talk to a much younger "you" about intimacy, sexuality, and relationships, what would you say?*

2. *Do you believe it's possible to refrain from sexual intimacy before or outside marriage? What would it take for you to do so?*

3. *Why do you think sexual regrets are so hard to overcome? What would you say to someone struggling to find forgiveness in this area?*

Suggested Action Steps:

1. *Have you seen your gynecologist recently? Do you need to discuss STDs or contraception? Make an appointment today.*

2. *Are there aspects of contraception or STDs about which you need to talk with your husband? Pray and plan for a time when you can address the issue.*

3. *If there are aspects of your sexual past for which you need God's forgiveness, find a time and place to be alone where you can pray. Read aloud 1 John 1:9 (see below). Or read about how Jesus treated the woman caught in adultery (John 8:2–11). Then pray this prayer: "Lord Jesus, I feel dirty and ashamed. Please forgive me for _____. I ask you to cleanse both my body and my*

soul. I ask you to make me clean and help me to walk with You in a new life. Amen."

Scripture to Contemplate or Memorize:

"If we confess our sins, he is faithful and just and will forgive us our sins and purify us from all unrighteousness." (1 John 1:9)

Chapter 20

What Makes a Marriage Work

JOHN AND ANN Betar, 102 and 98 years old, respectively, joyfully celebrated their eighty-first wedding anniversary on November 25, 2013, and earned the unofficial title "America's Longest Married Couple."[1] John shared his secret with ABC News: "Don't hold a grudge. Forgive each other. Live accordingly." Ann agreed: "We are very fortunate. It is unconditional love and understanding. We have had that. We consider it a blessing."

It does all of us good to view stories like that. We need to be reminded that a successful marriage doesn't just happen. It's the union of two imperfect people who learn what it is to truly love each other.

John and Ann hinted at something confirmed by research. The most important relational need for both men and women is unconditional love.[2] All of the other aspects of a relationship may be truly important, but only after this first need is met. That unconditional love provides the fuel needed for both of you to address the other important aspects of your relationship.

What does that look like? "Each of you should look not only to your own interests, but also to the interests of others" (Philippians 2:4). Al and I don't have a perfect marriage, but we have a very happy one. And I can honestly say that we're each more interested in and worried about the other than about ourselves. This isn't a put-on: it's how we really feel.

That kind of unselfish, unconditional love doesn't just happen. It's a decision, and it's a blessing from God. Experiencing God's love yourself will provide you with a supply of love to offer your husband. And my wish for you is that your husband will also experience God's love and thus have love to give to you.

Many husbands spell love somewhere between S-E-X and R-E-S-P-E-C-T. What means love to you is not necessarily identical to what means love to your husband. I can recommend two great resources to help you understand more about these differences, and how doing so can result in a happier, stronger marriage: *5 Love Languages*,[3] and *Love and Respect*.[4]

That kind of love sometimes involves work. The following describes what it looks like in the areas of expectations, friendship, and managing conflict.

Different Expectations

Connie expected Will to read the Bible and pray with her, as well as to make life interesting. When Will left in the morning without praying with her, and when he was too tired to do so later, she felt disappointed. When he was unhappy or confused she saw him as weak and unworthy of respect.

Will expected Connie to be sympathetic and understanding when he'd had a bad day and to keep him from being lonely. When Connie was moody or anxious he felt as though she was letting him down. He saw her as demanding more from him than he was able to give.

Your expectations of marriage are undoubtedly different from your spouse's. Even if you communicated well before marriage, the realities of your life together will challenge those expectations.

And you WILL be disappointed.

I don't mean that you have to be disappointed in your spouse. But something, or many things, about marriage will be different from what you expected.

Here are some questions to help get the two of you on the same page:

1. **What do you expect from your marriage?** What did you think life with your spouse would be like? What did you look forward to?

2. **In what area(s) are you disappointed?** Which of your expectations aren't being met? From where or what do you get that sinking feeling "Oh No! I'm stuck with this"?

3. **What do you want or need from your spouse right now?** Not all expectations can be met. Think realistically about what your spouse could give you now that would help.

No human being can meet all of your expectations. Only God can be everything! But in a healthy marriage both partners get many of their needs met much of the time. Talk about these issues together, being specific about what you want, and ask respectfully.

Then allow your spouse to ask you for what he needs. Do all you can to fulfill his needs and expectations, and your own disappointment will lessen or disappear.

Managing Conflict

The question isn't whether you'll face conflicts in your marriage but rather how you'll manage conflicts when they arise. Managing conflict well in marriage is a learned skill; no one knows how to do it automatically, but anyone can get better at it.

Couples can fight about money, religion, parenting, sex, in-laws, and a host of other subjects. Don't be surprised when you and your spouse see things differently.

Following are five important skills that will help when conflict arises:

1. **Cool off.** Trying to work things out when you're both emotionally "hot" won't be productive. If either of you needs some time, back off. Let the emotional temperature cool down before trying to talk further.

2. **Don't ignore the problem.** If you need to cool off, that's just step one. You must come back together and

talk things through. Choose a time and place to deal with the issue when both of you are rested and rational.

3. **Be honest.** State your point of view clearly, completely, and concisely. (Did you get that, ladies? Concise!) Don't hide your own feelings or try to manipulate the truth. Being honest is the only way to build a healthy relationship.

4. **Listen!** Spend as much time listening to his point of view as you do in sharing your own. Don't listen in order to find fault or debate; listen to fully understand where he's coming from.

5. **Push beyond discomfort.** Learning to fight fair may feel uncomfortable, vulnerable, and risky. Like any new skill, it takes practice. Don't quit until you learn how to sanely resolve conflicts together.

Conflicts don't magically resolve themselves just because you go to church every week or have a Bible on the table. Prayerfully ask God to help you work wisely on this aspect of your marriage.

Preserving Friendship

When you were dating, you easily came up with interesting things to do with your sweetheart. You looked forward to spending every possible moment together.

Now that you've been married for some years, you probably spend more time thinking about work, budgets, kids, schedules, and just getting through the day. You know date night is important, but it doesn't happen often enough. Preserving friendship with your husband means being intentional and deciding to do things that nurture that friendship.

Here are three ways in which you can nurture friendship together.

1. **Enter his world.** There are some things he enjoys that you don't. Stretch yourself and choose to joyfully spend time doing some of those things. Go golfing or fishing with him. Watch a movie he enjoys. Go along

on a business trip if you're able. As one husband said to his wife, "The afternoon you spent looking at fishing gear with me was the best gift you ever gave me."

2. **Invite him into your world.** Invite your husband to join you in some of the activities you enjoy. He may not always take you up on it, but the invitation makes him feel special. Ask him to go shopping with you, and limit the excursion to the amount of time he can tolerate. Invite him to visit your work, if appropriate. Let him get to know different aspects of yourself.

3. **Make memories together.** This is the most important of all, and it's always possible. Try something new, such as visiting a different restaurant, taking a class, or helping another family in need—together. Preserve a time at least twice a month to do something together, even if you don't have any money. Get creative if necessary, but just do it.

I want you to have a long and happy marriage.

Now quit reading this, go kiss your husband, and tell him "I LOVE YOU!"

Suggested Discussion Questions:

1. *Are disappointed expectations creating unhappiness in your marriage? What are you doing about them?*

2. *What happens when there's conflict between the two of you? Are you satisfied with your methods for resolving conflict?*

3. *How would you rate your marriage on the friendship scale? What can you do to become friends again?*

Suggested Action Steps:

1. *Think of something your husband enjoys. Do something this week to join him in that activity.*

2. *Plan a "date night" with your husband. Do something different; take a walk in a park you've never been to, shop for and cook a new meal together, or go somewhere new and just talk.*

3. *Pray for your husband. Take several minutes every day this week to talk to God about him, asking God to bless him in specific ways.*

Scripture to Contemplate or Memorize:

"Each of you should look not only to your own interests, but also to the interests of others." (Philippians 2:4)

Chapter 21

The What and How of Communication in Marriage

I LOOK FORWARD to board meetings!

The meetings I have in mind aren't the kind you typically think of when you hear that term. These board meetings may be short or long, fun or serious, superficial or deep. The agenda may cover topics such as prayer and gratitude, stress over money or health, fears or hopes about the future, children or grandchildren, or strategy in business and ministry.

Yes, I'm talking about the board meetings my husband, Al, and I hold nearly every night when we go to bed. We've done this ever since we were first married, and I can't imagine a successful, happy marriage without doing something similar. Sometimes those board meetings are full of laughter and playful teasing. At other times there've been filled with tears. If we're tired they may be very short.

One board meeting doesn't always solve every issue on the agenda; that isn't their purpose. But they make certain that we air everything between us before we go to sleep. We close the day knowing we're on the same side, facing the same issues shoulder to shoulder. We understand what's important to each other and usually end up feeling closer than ever.

That doesn't mean that we never disagree or have problems. But having almost daily board meetings means that no wall has a chance to grow between us. Communication keeps the space between us cleared of anything that might drive us apart.

Rules for Communication

You probably don't need to be told the importance of communication for a healthy marriage. But although good communication between husband and wife is vital, it may not seem easy.

Some people find conversation easier than others. The conventional wisdom for years was that women were more verbal than men. Dr. Louann Brizendine, author of *The Female Brain*[1], has been widely quoted as claiming that "a woman uses about 20,000 words per day while a man uses about 7,000." That claim has not stood up to further scrutiny. In 2007 a University of Arizona study showed that both men and women speak, on average, the same number of words each day: about 16,000.[2]

Of course how much individuals speak each day varies widely, based more on personality than on gender. Yes, men can talk too! And as his wife, you may be in the best position to help your husband navigate the world of marriage communication.

If communication between you and your husband has been difficult, here are some parameters to consider:

1. **Choose the time and place.** The moment he walks in from a difficult day at work is not the time to unload on your husband about a serious problem. You know him; if there's a potentially difficult discussion coming, choose a time and place when both of you will be best able to think clearly.

2. **Own your own feelings.** No one, not even your spouse, has the power to make you do or say or feel anything. So own up. Say "I feel frustrated," "I feel angry," "I feel sad," or "I feel worried." If your feelings are too explosive, take a break. Your brain will be much clearer, and your mouth much less destructive, when the emotional temperature is a little cooler.

3. **Take time to listen.** Your husband has the same right to his thoughts and feelings as you do. Be quiet long enough to hear him out. Stop talking long enough to listen—really listen—to what's going on with him. And if it isn't clear to you, ask questions.

4. **Schedule talk time.** Nightly board meetings may not be your style, but you do need a regular pattern of times for focused communication. Perhaps it's Saturday morning over coffee, or a weekly Sunday night strategy session. The important thing is that it's planned, regular, and frequent.

5. **Put away distractions.** Turn off the TV. If you have children, make sure they're occupied elsewhere. This is a time to give your full attention and energy to sharing and listening to each other. And if you tend to get distracted by your cell phone, it needs to get turned off too.

6. **Be a safe listener.** If you want to understand your husband, be a safe place for him to share himself. Present an open and welcoming heart; he'll be able to tell if you really want to hear him or are just waiting to hear something to criticize.

And one final tip: if your husband is like many men, his brain works better when he isn't hungry. See to it, if necessary, that he has something to eat, and communication will be much easier.

What do you talk about?

So you've scheduled a board meeting, but you can't think of anything to put on the agenda. If you and your husband aren't used to communicating, it may be difficult to get things started. If the air has often been silent between you, here are some conversation starters:

1. **Who are you?** Share a bit of yourself, and then ask him to do the same. Start with something simple, such as what you like and don't like. That may mean

anything: food, type of vacation, music, worship style, home or yard styles, TV shows, date activities, etc.

2. **What do you find difficult?** Perhaps it's a coworker's behavior, making a personal decision, a specific temptation, a frustrating habit, a negative emotional reaction, a behavior or attitude you learned as a child, etc.

3. **What are you afraid of?** It could be fear of failure, of not measuring up, of running out of money, of a certain person or situation, of sickness, of not being important, of getting older, of dying, of the future, etc.

4. **What do you dream about?** Maybe you dream of visiting a certain landmark, taking an adventure trip, accomplishing something specific, breaking a habit or addiction, learning or doing something new, etc.

5. **What do you remember?** Share memories of growing up—good or bad, memories of your early days together, of people you knew, of experiences you treasure or regret, as well as how you feel about those memories.

6. **What do you want to change?** Talk about what you would like to change in your marriage, your health habits, your life circumstances, your sex life, your parenting, your attitudes and emotions, your spiritual growth, etc.

7. **What do you see God doing?** Share how you feel about God, about church, what you hear God saying, where you see Him leading you and your family, what role you see God giving you in His kingdom both now and in the future, ways in which He's pressing you to mature or change, etc.

When you first knew each other you probably talked endlessly. You can do that again. Intentional communication is strong glue in a relationship. The organ of intimacy really is the ear!

I challenge you to schedule your next board meeting this week.

Your marriage will be stronger for it. And you might be surprised at how God uses your decision to intentionally connect with your husband.

Suggested Discussion Questions:

1. *How would you rate the quality of the communication between you and your spouse?*

2. *What are some things you wish you could talk about, but don't?*

3. *How good a listener are you? How good a listener would your spouse say you are?*

Suggested Action Steps:

1. *Write down the elements of a communication time that would appeal to your husband: time, place, setting, etc. This might be very simple, but be specific.*

2. *Write down three things you would like to share with your husband. Start with an "I" statement, such as: "I'm afraid about . . ." or "I would like to . . ."*

3. *Schedule a communication time with your spouse at some point during this week.*

Scripture to Contemplate or Memorize:

"Let your conversation be always full of grace, seasoned with salt, so that you may know how to answer everyone." (Colossians 4:6)

Chapter 22

When Marriage Doesn't Work: Infertility and Divorce

JENNIFER, ONE OF our radio listeners, wrote to me: "I was married at the age of 18 and divorced at 21 (physical abuse problem), and I felt I was a horrible failure. I used to lie on the floor, listening to classical music, and cry because I couldn't fix it, or him. It was a very hard time for me."

There is no easy way out of that kind of pain. Filing the court papers doesn't heal the wound in your heart. A legal divorce doesn't accomplish an emotional divorce, which can take much, much longer.

I'm going to try something dangerous. I'm going to write about something I've only observed at close hand, without having personally experienced it from the inside. I want to share my heart about facing a difficult or destructive marriage.

My fear is that someone in a dangerously destructive marriage will hear something in this chapter that encourages her to stay, or that someone who is unhappy will hear something in this chapter that encourages her to go when her marriage might have been saved.

But perhaps that struggle is exactly the context in which these thoughts can be helpful. I offer them with humility and the hope that you will find them encouraging.

I've been very close to some very destructive marriages:

- A family member's marriage marred by repeated infidelity and violence
- A good friend whose husband abandoned her while she was pregnant—twice
- Several (friends and patients) whose marriages ended because of pornography
- Another family member whose marriage was destroyed by substance abuse
- Someone I know well whose marriage couldn't survive mental illness

If you're wrestling with a painful or destructive marriage, you know all too well the frustration, tears, and loneliness involved. You know the feelings of powerlessness, shame, sadness, disappointment, or guilt. You may have prayed, cried, and done all you could, only to be left with weariness and hopelessness.

There are two things I know for sure:

1. **God can heal anything.** That means you, and your marriage.

2. **Not every marriage can be saved.** That isn't because of any failure on God's part. But marriage involves two human beings, and you can't control your spouse.

Many Christian women have remained in destructive marriages because of guilt, trying to honor God, or following what their church teaches about the sinfulness of divorce. Others have left marriages simply because they were deeply unhappy, believing that God's primary desire for them is their happiness.

Neither of those options is consistent with Who God is or what He wants for His children. Only God can fully answer your questions. But you aren't alone, and you aren't the first person to wrestle with a destructive marriage.

Here are some points to consider in evaluating your situation:

1. **Unhappy and destructive are two different things.** A marriage in which you or your children are physically abused, emotionally traumatized, or sexually exploited is very different from a marriage in which you're sad, unfulfilled, or lonely. It's important for you to be honest about what is or isn't really going on in your marriage.

2. **Divorce doesn't end the pain.** If you choose to end your marriage, the pain won't end when the papers are signed. Emotional and spiritual healing will take much longer and may even be much harder. Especially if children are involved, the challenges are likely to continue indefinitely.

3. **Forgiveness doesn't always mean allowing yourself (or your children) to continue being hurt.** You can let your spouse off the hook and still get and stay away. Forgiveness is a matter of the heart, between you and God. It's a separate question from whether it's safe or wise to stay married.

4. **You aren't alone.** Even if you feel as though you are. God sees you, and He understands. There are many others who've experienced what you're experiencing and can offer insight, encouragement, and support. Connecting with others is vital to your healing, whether or not you're married.

5. **It takes two to tangle.** There are two sides to every story, and certainly two in every marriage. You've made mistakes. Your spouse has made mistakes. Which of you has made the most mistakes is NOT a deciding factor in whether or not to end your marriage.

6. **You'll have to change, whether or not you stay married.** To heal a troubled marriage will take some change on your part, not just your spouse's. To heal after a destructive marriage ends will take some real change as well. The only option that doesn't involve

scary change is staying in the same destructive marriage you're in now.

7. **You'll need God's intervention, whether or not your marriage ends.** God's grace is the only thing that will heal your troubled marriage (if you stay) or your troubled heart (whether you leave or stay). You can't walk this journey alone. You may have prayed before; if so, keep on praying. You NEED God with you, no matter what happens with your marriage.

How Do I Decide?

Is your marriage too destructive to save?

I don't know. But God does. Here are two questions for you to think and pray through. I believe that process, with God's help, will give you the answer to whether or not your marriage is too destructive to save.

1. **Am I allowing God to do what He needs to do with me?** If your marriage ends, you'll want to look back and know that you did everything within your power to make things work. Being honest about your own roll, and allowing God to work on you, is all you can control. "If it is possible, as much as depends on you, live peaceably with all men" (Romans 12:18).

2. **Is my spouse willing to allow God to do what He needs to do with him?** This is the part you can't control, but you must be brutally honest about the answer. And that answer will come from his actions, not his words. God can heal marriages marred by violence, infidelity, and/or addiction, but only if BOTH partners are committed to allowing Him to do so. You can't force your husband to change. You can only be honest about whether or not his habitual actions are truly destructive and whether his present actions demonstrate a commitment to doing whatever it takes to change.

If your husband's actions are truly destructive, and if you've done all within your power to make things work and he isn't demonstrating change, it's time to seriously pray about getting out. And to take action.

God has a future for you. It's OK to step into that future. Know that He will be there with you, married or not.

Finding Healing

Whether you leave or stay, God wants to bring you healing.

Jennifer has now been happily married again for more than 40 years, but healing didn't come easily. She wrote: "I learned how to forgive!! I really did. . . . Life is amazing, isn't it? Forgiveness came easy once I found the Holy Spirit." Jennifer recognized that it was the Holy Spirit who worked forgiveness in her heart. That's really the only way it's possible.

Does God want you happy? I prefer to say God wants you healed. Whether that's to happen within or outside your marriage only you and God can determine. But I know He can do it for you.

Suggested Discussion Questions:

1. *What examples of destructive marriages have you seen or perhaps experienced?*

2. *What do you believe are "big enough" reasons for leaving a marriage?*

3. *Have you wrestled with the question of whether or not your marriage can be saved? How do you know whether it's truly destructive or "simply" seriously unhappy?*

Suggested Action Steps:

1. *Pretend you are yourself 20 years from now. Look back on your current marriage and write a letter to yourself. What advice would you give?*

2. *Have you asked God what He sees when He looks at*

your marriage? Ask Him now, and spend some time listening for His answer.

3. *Get some help. This has never been easier. If your safety is in jeopardy, call the Domestic Violence Hotline: 1-800-799-SAFE, or check out www.thehotline.org. It's free, confidential, and nonjudgmental.*

Scripture to Contemplate or Memorize:

"You hear, O Lord, the desire of the afflicted; you encourage them, and you listen to their cry, defending the fatherless and the oppressed, in order that man, who is of the earth, may terrify no more." (Psalm 10:17,18)

Chapter 23

Do's and Don'ts for Wives on Placing God First

DENISE, A YOUNG wife and a new Christian, asked me, "How can I respect and love my husband while making God first in my life? Isn't my husband supposed to be Number One? But does that mean I'm not honoring God as I should? I'm confused."

I'm sure Denise isn't the only one who is sometimes confused. If you're a woman who wants to honor both God and your husband, how do you go about doing that? Who comes first? God comes first, right? But what does that do to your husband's heart? You want him to be the spiritual head of your home, don't you? How can he be your spiritual head and also a competitor with God for your heart?

God never intended this to be confusing. He intended for the Christian life to bring husband and wife closer together, not drive them apart.

If your husband is demanding you do something that would compromise your Christian walk, or that is clearly against God's laws, then you must obey God. And if your husband isn't walking with God, there may be times when you feel torn between doing what your husband wants (i.e., drinking, shady business dealing, etc.) and what would honor God. And of course you know where your first loyalty must lie.

But the majority of the time the situation doesn't involve either/or, one or the other. You honor God by respecting and loving your husband. I remember another young wife who said, "I was upstairs praying in our room and clearly heard God say to me, 'Stop praying, go downstairs, and make love to your husband.'" Yes, God cares a great deal about how you go about keeping your marriage strong.

A few do's and don'ts that may help:

- **DON'T** depend on your husband for all your spiritual needs. God will work through him to bless you. But your strength and fulfillment come directly from God, not from your husband.

- **DON'T** endlessly talk about Jesus in front of your husband as though He were your boyfriend. God works differently in men's and women's hearts; respect your husband enough to understand how that might make him feel.

- **DON'T** use your spiritual activities as an excuse to avoid spending time with your husband. Prayer, Bible study, and church involvement are important, but just as important are the times you focus directly on your relationship with the man God gave you.

- **DON'T** expect God to work in your husband's life in exactly the same way He works in yours. Be alert to what God is doing in his heart. Be supportive, not nagging, when it comes to his spiritual growth.

- **DON'T** display your spiritual prowess in an attempt to show him up. Believe me, he'll pick up on your attitude if you think you're more spiritually advanced than he is. And this will totally turn him off—from you, and possibly even from God.

And now, a few suggestions for things you can do:

- **DO** consistently search for ways by which you can show your husband how much you both respect and love him. Give him no reason, ever, to question either your love or your respect.

- **DO** spend your own time with God. Pray for your husband. Pray for your own heart; that's the way you get your own soul filled up. Spend time listening to what God says to you about how to relate to your husband.

- **DO** find ways to serve your husband, and do it as though you're serving the Lord. Be assured that you're pleasing God just as much when you cook his favorite meal or connect with him sexually as when you pray for him.

- **DO** share your spiritual journey with him. One of the ways you can help your husband is by letting him see what Jesus means to you in real and practical ways. God may use you to draw your husband closer to Himself.

- **DO** honor your husband's spiritual journey. Your job isn't Junior Holy Spirit: you're his wife. Relish the joy of that role. You don't have to change him. When opportunities arise, join hands (literally or figuratively) in following God together.

Honoring and loving God should lead you to honor and love your husband more than ever. You'll both be glad you do.

Husband as Spiritual Head of the Home

But what about the husband being the head of the home (Ephesians 5:23), especially in a spiritual sense? Many Christian women complain that their husbands aren't fulfilling their godly duty of being the spiritual head of the household. They envy women whose husbands seem more spiritual. Their disappointment can lead to conflict, anger, and emotional separation in the marriage.

Some women have an idealized picture of what their marriage should be, especially when it comes to the spiritual aspect. They imagine their husband gathering the family daily for prayer and Bible reading. They expect him to be the energy impetus behind going to church and to speak wisely about what God says. They want him to identify and share areas in which she (and the children) need spiritual growth and help them experience that growth.

Living up to that idealized picture is a tall order for any man. And I'm not sure that's really what God meant when He commended Abraham "that he may command his children and his household after him, that they keep the way of the Lord" (Genesis 18:19).

Yes, God entrusts husbands and fathers with a huge responsibility. But the picture many women have has become feminized. Nowhere does God say that you, as a wife, are to nag and cajole and shame your husband into certain spiritual practices. It just doesn't work!

That said, you can be a tremendous help to your husband in fulfilling what God has given him to do. Here are some suggestions:

1. **Respect your husband's personality.** Don't assume he'll demonstrate his walk with God in the same way you do, or the way some other man does. God works in each person's heart in a way their personality can understand and to which it can respond.

2. **Respect God's work in your husband's life.** Remember that your husband is accountable first to God, not to you. Be alert to the ways God is working in his life. Celebrate any changes you see God working in him.

3. **Encourage what you want more of.** Many men naturally want a happy wife and are more likely on that basis to do what pleases her. When he makes an effort to pray, read Scripture, or some other spiritual practice you find fulfilling, let him know how much this means to you.

4. **Pray for your husband daily.** Oh, the power of a praying wife! How many husbands have been brought closer to God through the prayers of the person closest to them. Don't give up.

5. **Respect your husband's spiritual lead.** If your husband voices a spiritual need or desire, go along if at all possible. If he hears something from God about the direction of your marriage or family, do your best to respect and honor that.

God desires your husband's whole heart even more than you do. Pray that you will help that happen rather than getting in the way.

And remember that God has a purpose not only for you individually but also for your marriage and family. There's nothing more exciting than to experience God using your marriage to benefit His kingdom.

Suggested Discussion Questions:

1. *How do you think your husband would respond if asked, "Does your wife help or hinder the spiritual climate in your home?"*

2. *Do you face any conflict between God's having first place in your heart and still fully loving and respecting your husband? If so, how do you manage that conflict?*

3. *How have you shared your spiritual journey with your husband? How has doing so impacted your relationship?*

Suggested Action Steps:

1. *Write down several things you see God doing in your husband's life, or trying to do. What can you do to support God's working in him?*

2. *Write down all the ways you can think of in which your husband helps your marriage or family spiritually. Tell him how much you appreciate his efforts.*

3. *Have you tried to be Junior Holy Spirit to your husband? If so, ask God and your husband for forgiveness.*

Scripture to Contemplate or Memorize:

"How do you know, wife, whether you will save your husband? Or, how do you know, husband, whether you will save your wife?" (1 Corinthians 7:16)

Chapter 24

Especially for Men: What Women Wish They Knew

GARY HAD BEEN frustrated one too many times with his wife, Jelissa. If he heard the words "I'm just hormonal" one more time—well, there was no telling what might happen. After trying to work off his frustration at the gym, he confided to his friend Chris in the locker room, "It'll be another two weeks before we have any peace at our house. And intimacy is out of the question. I never know what mood she'll be in when I come home. Nothing I do is ever enough good enough for her. I just give up!"

Through our various media programs I hear from as many men as I do women. When it comes to the women in their lives, they often talk about feeling confused, frustrated, powerless, angry, hopeless, rejected, and empty.

Most of this book is written especially for women. So if you're a guy reading this, it's likely the woman in your life has suggested that you read this chapter. I hope you're in love, satisfied, grateful, and happy with your relationship. But if you're less than satisfied, I hope to give you an inside view into the sometimes confusing female soul and help you discover what you can do to make things better.

One frustrated husband said, "If a woman is upset, hold her and tell her how beautiful she is. If she starts to growl, retreat to a safe distance and throw chocolate at her." Ever feel like that?

Let me make one thing clear: your wife is 100% responsible for her own behavior, hormonal or not. Much of the rest of this book is written to help her take responsibility for her attitudes and actions, including how she responds to you. So don't feel as though she's getting off the hook.

But to help you avoid feeling sorry for yourself or looking outside your marriage for satisfaction, this chapter will focus on five things you as a man can do to make things better between the two of you.

1. **Your wife needs to FEEL loved by you.** It isn't because she doesn't believe you love her; it's just the way she's made. Your wife encounters many messages throughout the day that tend to make her feel tired, ugly, old, and not good enough. She needs your consistent reassurance of how much you love her in order to provide a counterattack to the negative messages she picks up from other sources. And that reassurance will make her want to be close to you.

   What you can do: It helps to know what her love language is.[1] If she needs love notes, taking out the garbage won't do the trick. If she needs focused time with you, a long, affectionate kiss won't be enough. Speak "I love you" to her in the language she can understand. (And by the way, I give her the same advice about showing her love to you!)

2. **Your wife's hormonal nature is more complicated than yours.** As if you didn't know that already! A women goes through numerous hormonal changes during different life stages, some of which significantly affect her emotionally and sexually. Other medical problems or medication side effects can also affect her this way. A woman's sexual response is more complicated than a man's, and when she feels uptight or unresponsive she herself doesn't always know for sure what's wrong.

What you can do: Simply understanding that it isn't all your fault can help ease your frustration. And sometimes you do need to allow your wife some grace in this area. That said, it's OK to hold her accountable in the sense of letting her know the effect her behavior may be having on you. Encourage her to see a doctor if she needs to. Your love and support will mean a lot, and sometimes your support in the area of seeking help will make all the difference.

3. **Your wife needs your godly leadership.** Some women may yell at me for saying this, but it's true, and it's biblical. It's never OK for you to become authoritarian or abusive, or to hurt her. The truth is, your wife can probably do some things better than you can. But she needs you to be the buffer against the "big bad world out there," to stand up and be her protector and provider, to shoulder much of the heaviness of life, and to do what you can to provide a place within which she can thrive.

    What you can do: God calls on you to unselfishly love your wife (Ephesians 5:25–28), not because she deserves it but because that's how God is. Your wife will often rise to the level at which you see her. If you value and cherish her even more than yourself, she'll be inclined to display her beauty to you—physically, emotionally, and spiritually.

4. **Your wife wants intimacy too.** It just may be that you spell intimacy S-E-X and that she's more likely to spell it T-A-L-K. Yes, you have sexual needs, and yes, your wife is 100% responsible for how she responds to you. But think of her as a flower; it typically takes gently peeling back each petal, sometimes through conversation, sometimes through physical touch, to reach her heart. Your reward for patience and gentleness is the sweetness within, both physically and spiritually.

What you can do: Foreplay doesn't start when you crawl into bed at night; it starts with all the little things you do and say all day. A woman needs to feel desired, thought about, cherished, and cared for. She'll sense whether you want only her body or if you truly care about HER. Stretch yourself and find a way to romance your wife. You were creative when you dated her; do it again! You're like God when you woo your wife and help her respond to you (Hosea 2:14).

5. **You are responsible first to God.** And so is your wife. You have failed her, and she has failed you. Only with God's grace, forgiveness, and transforming power can any two sinful people enjoy a long and successful marriage. God made you the way you are, with all your needs, strengths, and even vulnerabilities. And He knows exactly what you need in order to grow, thrive, and fulfill your purpose in His kingdom.

   What you can do: Take your own spiritual life seriously. Get together with other Christian men and help each other live with sexual integrity. (Check out Every Man's Battle.[2]) Observe your wife's spiritual journey, and learn together whenever you can. Let God be the glue that holds you together and changes you both.

You won your wife's heart once. Wouldn't you like to do it again? Wouldn't you like her to look at you the way she did when you first said "I Do"?

I'll let you in on a little secret. We women don't want you to win our heart only once; we want you to keep on winning it, over and over again. We want you to be our hero again and again. Don't waste time wondering whether this is fair or unfair: it's just the way a woman's heart works.

If you want to be irresistible to your wife, treat her as the most valuable thing in your world. Study your wife. Cherish her for who she is, and not just her body. And she'll be much more likely to respond with respect, love, and intimacy.

Suggested Discussion Questions:

1. *For women: Are these the most important points you wish men—or your man in particular—knew about you? Anything else?*

2. *For men: Do these points in some way help you understand how your wife has responded to you?*

Suggested Action Steps:

1. *Women: Suggest that the man in your life read this chapter. Then talk about it together.*

2. *Men: Ask your wife how you're doing on the elements mentioned in this chapter. Her perspective may help you see how you can make things better between the two of you.*

Scripture to Contemplate or Memorize:

"So husbands ought to love their own wives as their own bodies; he who loves his wife loves himself." (Ephesians 5:28)

Part Three

HEALTHY SPIRITUALITY

"This is the covenant I will make with the house of Israel after that time, declares the Lord. I will put my laws in their minds and write them on their hearts. I will be their God, and they will be my people." (HEBREWS 8:10)

"Pray as though everything depended on God. Work as though everything depended on you."

(SAINT AUGUSTINE)

Chapter 25

Why Spirituality Matters for Your Health

JANICE AND I met for the first time at her first prenatal visit. After all the usual health questions I asked, "Have you ever been pregnant before?" And that started a flood of tears. Yes, she had been pregnant before, four times. And she'd had four abortions. She felt so guilty for having ended her other pregnancies and was now determined to have this baby.

I reminded Janice that God is a God of new beginnings. I told her I was proud of her for deciding to have this baby and assured her that God felt the same way. He would be with her through all the challenges of bringing this child into the world, and this child had a special place in God's plan.

I could have responded to Janice in a number of different ways that day. I could have told her that although having several previous abortions might slightly increase the risks to her current pregnancy, most of the time someone like her could expect to deliver a healthy baby. I could have offered her a referral to a mental health provider to deal with her anxiety. And those things would have been appropriate.

But what Janice needed most at that moment was a way to deal with the heaviness of her guilt. She needed to hear that God wasn't out to punish her but would rejoice with her as she brought this child into the world. His forgiveness is real, and He would gladly walk with her into her future.

Martin Luther reportedly agonized over the state of his soul to the point of becoming physically ill. Where we stand in our relationship with God has much to do with our overall state of health. Faith is a journey that continues throughout life, and it's worth paying attention to.

Like any relationship, our connection with God isn't static. And it can be healthy or unhealthy. God designed us to be in intimacy with Himself, but that truth has often been badly distorted by people who claim to be speaking in His name.

Perhaps the whole idea of spiritual health is distasteful to you right now. Perhaps you've experienced some unhealthy spirituality that has turned you off. You may have seen people who professed to be following God act in ways that were anything but godly. The Sunday school teacher spends Friday night in a bar, drinking. The Christian family man cheats his customers and competitors whenever he can. The pastor gets caught cheating on his wife. The good-looking Christian wife is known for being selfish, angry, and manipulative. An evangelist is found to be misusing donated funds. Who would want to be around these people?

And even more to the point, who would want to be like them? Why not just walk away from this whole "Christian" thing and do what I want?

Is Spirituality "Good for You"?

You might have expected me to claim that Christianity or, more generically, spirituality is a good thing for your health. But that isn't what I believe.

And both science and God's Word back me up on this.

Now before you throw this book away, think of it like this. The way spirituality impacts your health isn't unlike the way other relationships affect you. If your relationships with your husband, children, family, and friends are relatively healthy, then of course these interconnections benefit your health. We've just spent several chapters talking about that. But if your relationships are characterized by violence, addiction, anger, and conflict, than your physical, emotional, and spiritual health will be seriously damaged.

It's the same with your spiritual life. Numerous studies point to a pattern: a relatively healthy spirituality is associated with lessened anxiety and depression, a better quality of life, positive stress-related growth, less chronic pain, and lower mortality. On the other hand, negative spirituality is associated with poorer physical health, increased mortality, increased anxiety and depression, lower self-esteem, and a heightened incidence of post-traumatic stress disorder.[1]

And what does God have to say about this? Religious words and practices in themselves may be worthless! "The LORD says: 'These people come near to me with their mouth and honor me with their lips, but their hearts are far from me. Their worship of me is made up only of rules taught by men'" (Isaiah 29:13).

So what IS healthy spirituality?

There has been quite a lot of scientific research on that question, and we'll comment a little more in some of the coming chapters. But here's a great summary by Dr. Kenneth Pargament, Professor of Psychology at Bowling Green University:

> *Some forms of religion are more helpful than others. A religion that is internalized, intrinsically motivated, and built on a belief in a greater meaning in life, a secure relationship with God, and a sense of spiritual connectedness with others has positive implications for well-being. Conversely, a religion that is imposed, unexamined, and reflective of a tenuous relationship with God and the world bodes poorly for well-being.*[2]

God would agree. He doesn't care nearly as much about your religious behaviors as He does about your well-being and the status of your heart. Here's a short list, from the Bible, of what God is looking for from you:

1. **Your listening.** Like it or not, He's smarter than you. And that's in all ways a good thing! He's looking for you to listen, not just with your ears but with your actions as well: "Be doers of the word, and not hearers only, deceiving yourselves" (James 1:22).

2. **Your allegiance.** God's enemy declared war against

Him long before you and I came along. And whether or not we want to, each one of us must choose sides in this war. "Choose for yourselves this day whom you will serve. . . . But as for me and my house, we will serve the Lord" (Joshua 24:15).

3. **Your trust.** Is God worthy of your trust? Will He do what He says He'll do? Can you live your life based on what He says? That's what faith is all about, and it's what truly pleases God. "But without faith it is impossible to please Him" (Hebrews 11:6).

4. **Your worship.** Today we call our idols by almost any other name: entertainment, popularity, convenience, material possessions, other people's opinions, or any of a wide-ranging number of other possibilities. God expects to come first, and He deserves to. In Jesus' own words, "For it is written: 'Worship the Lord your God, and serve him only'" (Matthew 4:10).

5. **Your transformation.** God loves you unreservedly, just the way you are. But He also loves you too much to let you remain in your broken down, sinful condition. He asks you to let Him transform you from the inside out, "that he might sanctify and cleanse [the church] with the washing of water by the word" (Ephesians 5:26).

6. **Your love.** Not a "peck-on-the-cheek" kind of love, but an intense, loyal, intimate, passionate love that causes you to leave behind all lesser lovers and devote your life to following wherever He leads. And then to pass that love along. "Love the Lord your God with all your heart and with all your soul and with all your strength and with all your mind" and "Love your neighbor as yourself" (Luke 10:27).

So yes, your spiritual life makes a huge impact on your health in every way. And understanding what God wants most from you will make sure the impact is positive.

Suggested Discussion Questions:

1. *Most people have seen or experienced some negative impact of religion or spirituality. How about you? If so, what was that like?*

2. *What are some characteristics of "bad" religion, the kind that negatively impacts one's life? What are some characteristics of "good" religion, the kind that results in a positive impact?*

3. *What do you believe God wants from you?*

Suggested Action Steps:

1. *Look back at your own experience of religion and/or spirituality? Has it helped you or hurt you? Write about your answer.*

2. *Read some of the Scriptures mentioned in this chapter, along with the surrounding verses for their context. Do the insights you glean from these verses change your picture of God in some way?*

3. *Imagine one thing you can do this week to give God something He wants from you (an item from the short list). Follow through on that prompt.*

Scripture to Contemplate or Memorize:

"He answered: 'Love the Lord your God with all your heart and with all your soul and with all your strength and with all your mind.' . . . 'Love your neighbor as yourself.'" (Luke 10:27)

Chapter 26

Making Scripture Work

I WILL ALWAYS remember a time some years ago when I found myself in a difficult situation that could have been dangerous for me, both physically and spiritually. I struggled momentarily with how to proceed. But then out of my mouth came the same words 12-year-old Jesus said: "I must be about my Father's business" (Luke 2:49). Those words diffused the situation, and I was spared both the physical and spiritual pain that could have resulted.

That may sound like a strange story, but I can assure you it's true. Nothing like that had happened to me before, nor have I experienced anything similar since. Why those words at that moment? I know that Scripture was in my heart because of the time I had spent reading the Bible. I have never been more grateful for God's Word in my life. It was truly a moment when Jesus' promise was fulfilled: "Say whatever is given you at the time, for it is not you speaking, but the Holy Spirit" (Mark 13:11).

Lest you think I'm some kind of super-spiritual saint who has memorized most of the New Testament and has a Bible verse for every situation, I assure you that I'm not. I was blessed to start reading the Bible regularly when I was a child. But there have been periods of time when Bible reading hasn't been a daily part of my life. Even today I have to actively discipline myself to spend time with the Bible daily, and I don't do it perfectly.

But after being literally saved from harm by words from Scripture, as I related above, I'm all the more convinced that God wants to take the Bible and change our lives through it.

We won't get into a theological discussion on why the Bible is the Word of God, talk about the amazing historical realities involved in its preservation, or address the accusations made by some that there are mistakes in the Bible. I want to help you make the Bible "work." I want you to experience the role it can play in your everyday life, to see how God can use it in truly miraculous ways for you.

The Problem

So that little voice in your head is nudging "Read the Bible!" Intellectually, you accept the fact that for you as a Christian reading the Bible would be a good thing to do.

But you don't feel like it. You're tired. The Bible seems too difficult to understand. You don't know where to start. Last time you tried you got bogged down in a long list of names, dates, and numbers. It seems as though the historical events related in the Bible happened a long time ago, and it's a real stretch for you to make them mean something for today. And then there's the possibility that if you did read and benefit from God's Word, you might find something in your lifestyle that you'd have to change, and you aren't ready for that unwelcome consequence. Besides, so many people disagree on what the Bible really means, so who's to say?

On the other hand, maybe you're one of those who has read and studied the Bible a great deal. You know a lot about its original writing and the circumstances behind each writer's contribution. But your soul is tired because every time you try reading your mind kicks into high intellectual gear trying to figure out something new or thinking of something you need to study.

The Bible is a collection of stories, poems, letters, prophecy, wisdom principles, and other literary forms written by many authors over many years. But it's so much more than that as well. God intends for the Bible to be His letter directly to you. It's a big part of how He works to change you from the inside out.

There are two primary approaches to reading the Bible, and both are helpful and important.

1. **Study the Bible.** You read a passage of Scripture, use Bible study helps to aid you in researching the original setting and language, look for comparable and complementary passages of Scripture, and come to a conclusion on what the writing meant for its original audience and what it means for readers today. There are numerous Bible study tools available now, many free on the internet.[1] Study of the Bible in this way is more of an intellectual pursuit—interesting and important for understanding, but not always life-changing.

2. **Read the Bible for food.** You invite the Holy Spirit to take a passage of Scripture and make it real to you. You read in order to feed your soul, to hear from God, to nurture your spirit, and to allow God to use its words to transform you from the inside out. You obtain comfort, peace, guidance, hope, joy, courage, wisdom, and love from your time in the Bible. It's impossible to read the Bible in this way and remain unchanged.

It's reading for spiritual food that really makes the difference. Study is good, and it has its place, but it's the spiritual food that will change you.

What to Do with the Bible

If you don't feel like reading the Bible, or aren't used to making it a part of your day, allow me to suggest some ways to begin reading for spiritual food.

1. **Pray about it.** Let God know how you feel—weary, guilty, nervous, frustrated, anxious, or confused. Ask Him to guide you to the Scripture portion you need to read and to make those verses mean something to your soul.

2. **Try listening.** If reading is difficult, try listening to an audio Bible. I love the free YouVersion® Bible app[2]; it

provides a way for you to keep the Bible with you always, and some entire versions are available in audio.

3. **Start with the story of Jesus.** If you're new to the Bible, or are stuck in a rut, this is one of the two best places to start reading. Choose one of the Gospels, perhaps John, and read a story each day. Imagine yourself in the story.

4. **Start with the psalms.** This is another excellent place to start or restart your reading. Many of the psalms are prayers, and they express every different human emotion. You're sure to find one or more that expresses what's in your heart.

5. **Take it in bite-sized pieces.** Read a few verses, a story, a psalm, or a chapter, and then pause and think. If you feel in danger of developing soul indigestion, stop and do it again tomorrow.

6. **Don't overthink.** This approach to Bible reading is for spiritual food, not intellectual stimulation. Serious Bible study is important, but that's for another time. Let your heart take the time to absorb a small portion at a time.

7. **Ask, "What is God saying to me?"** Part of the mystery of God's Holy Spirit is the way in which He takes words from Scripture and does something in your heart with them. Give Him a chance to do so.

If all you have is a few minutes a day, that's enough to begin. Make it happen while you're driving to work, while your child is taking a nap, or while you're drinking your morning coffee.

I hope this gives you an idea for how you can begin to allow the Bible to be part of your daily life. Engaging with God's Word is a way of entering God's presence and giving Him a chance to change you (see 2 Corinthians 3:18).

Just as with human relationships, the rewards come with ongoing commitment. When I look back, I can see the tremendous difference my commitment to reading the Bible has made in my life. And I know you'll find the same.

Keep at it. I can guarantee you that God will make something happen in your life because of it.

Suggested Discussion Questions:

1. *When you read the Bible, are you typically reading for study or for spiritual food? What do you think about the difference between those two methods?*

2. *Can you think back to a time when your Bible reading has made a significant difference in your life? Talk about it.*

3. *What are some ways in which you could make the Bible a more regular part of your daily life?*

Suggested Action Steps:

1. *Download the free YouVersion® Bible app on your smartphone. Register for one of the reading plans available.*

2. *If you aren't already reading the Bible daily, work into your schedule one specific time each day this week when you can spend a few minutes with the Bible. Set your phone alarm if necessary to remind you.*

3. *Explore some of the free online Bible study guides. Bookmark one or more sites you can come back to when you have a question about something you read.*

Scripture to Contemplate or Memorize:

"When your words came, I ate them; they were my joy and my heart's delight, for I bear your name, O Lord God Almighty." (Jeremiah 15:16)

Chapter 27

What Prayer Is All About

THE FOLLOWING STORY is shared by Dennis and Barbara Rainey.[1] And I can't think of any better way to open this chapter about prayer.

> Tommy was a National Guard Reservist called into action during the Gulf War. On the last Sunday before his actual deployment, the church he attended had a special time of prayer, sending him off with their promise of support and encouragement.
>
> As you can imagine, the prayers for Tommy's safety were thick with theology and high-sounding words (as churchy prayers often are): "Sovereign God of the universe, we trust that You will protect this young man on his mission, O Lord, and that You will keep him within the shelter of Your wings." All very sincere, I'm sure, but quite flowery and unoriginal.
>
> Then a little eight-year-old voice piped up from the back, "Dear Jesus, don't let Tommy get killed, okay? That's all. Okay. Amen."

I think God smiles at the kind of prayers that eight-year-old child prayed. That's the kind of prayer that touches His heart. So no big theological discussion here; just some thoughts on making this thing called prayer work.

Do you ever get more than a little frustrated, as I do, with some Christian types who seem to so easily speak wonderful, spiritual-sounding phrases when they need to, while the rest of the time acting anything but Christlike? A few King James phrases on Sunday morning or a memorized but thoughtless prayer at bedtime won't cut it.

Prayer isn't a performance; it's a conversation. And if you're like the majority of women, you can do "conversation" quite well. Think of all the text messages, phone calls, Instagram pictures, Facebook updates, sticky notes, and emails you send and receive in an average day. And then there's meeting with a friend for coffee, the long phone call with an old classmate, a girls' night out for fun, and the intimate gaze-into-your-eyes dinner for two. You know how to communicate.

Why not see prayer in the same way?

- Send God a text message: "That's beautiful! Thank You!" or "Ouch! Can You help me out here?"

- Meet God for coffee. Open your day together. Share your thoughts with Him, and hear His plans for today as well.

- Plan an intimate "dinner for two." Carve out a couple of hours where it's just you and Him. Bare your soul to Him. Be silent and hear His heart for you, your future, and your world.

I'm sure you can think of many different ways in which you communicate throughout the course of your day; think of how each one of those ways can be analogous to a way in which you communicate with God.

Ways to Experience Prayer

There are many different ways to experience prayer. Here are five, in no particular order:

1. **"God, Help Me! Please!"** Who better to turn to when you're in trouble than God! A child in trouble, a physical illness, financial pressure, anxiety, fear, loneliness, pain—bring it all to Him. He's the only One

with big enough shoulders to carry it all. Sometimes it's a momentary desperate cry, as with that eight-year old child asking for Tommy to not get killed. Sometimes it's a whole list of needs you carry to Him. Sometimes it's an emotional outpouring from the overwhelming pain in your soul. It's turning to Him in your need, whatever that is.

2. **Listening for His Voice.** Communication is only communication when it goes both ways. And that holds true with God as well. Sometimes it's important to just sit quietly, silent in His presence. If there's something specific on your heart, ask Him to talk to you about that specific thing. Then be quiet and listen.

   The other voices in your soul can easily drown out His voice. So if your mind is screaming, find ways to become quiet. That may mean a worship setting, a place in nature, or calming music. If your own emotions are screaming, you may need to spill them out to Him first before you can be calm and hear Him in your spirit.

3. **Praying with Others.** My husband and I pray aloud in our home daily; I've discovered this to be one of the most bonding and healing things we do together. In the same way, corporate prayer within the body of Christ is a big part of why we come together as God's people. There's something very powerful about a group of Christians gathering in God's presence with a common purpose, inviting Him to make His kingdom real in their midst, their home, their church, their town, their world. Look for opportunities to pray with others.

4. **Praying for Others.** Lifting up others before God, either in your private prayers or publicly, is simply an outflow of God's Spirit working within you. There's nothing more exhilarating than seeing God act in someone else's life after you've prayed for Him to do so. Start with the people closest to you, your family

and friends. But don't stop there; include your coworkers, Facebook friends, church family, community, and other groups and individuals God places on your heart.

5. **Taking God into Everyday Life.** Sometimes I pray quietly while performing a difficult medical procedure or struggling with a hard decision. God wants to be part of your life every hour of the day, and you can talk to Him about it. Sometimes the words may be heard and understood by God alone, but your overture opens your heart to Him and brings Him directly into your circumstances. That honors Him. And it helps keep your heart from going in dangerous or sinful directions as well.

If one single attitude has transformed my prayer life more than any other, it's been learning to listen. It's relatively easy to come to God begging and pleading, ready with a list of requests or even demands. But that would be like trying to develop a friendship or a romance when all you did was ask for things.

Instead, try sharing your life with God, talking to Him about anything and everything that matters to you, and inviting Him into your world. As your relationship with Him deepens, your prayer life will become even richer.

God is eager to both hear from you and talk to you. Talk with Him today.

Suggested Discussion Questions:

1. *Name several different ways in which you communicate on a regular basis. Include both the superficial and the intimate. How can each of those ways illustrate a kind of prayer?*

2. *How does listening for God's voice become part of prayer? What does that look like for you?*

3. *Think back to a time of prayer, either personal or corporate, that was especially meaningful for you. What made it so?*

Suggested Action Steps:

1. *Read through several of the shorter psalms. Notice the depth and range of emotions that are demonstrated. Make a note of some of those emotions.*

2. *Spend 15 minutes alone, silent, in God's presence. Set a timer if you need to, and play some quiet worship music if you wish. Begin with praying, "God, I'm here, and I'm listening." Then be quiet and listen.*

3. *Choose an alert to remind you to call out a short prayer to God during the day. Set your phone alarm or pick an activity, such as using the restroom, that you can use as a reminder.*

Scripture to Contemplate or Memorize:

"In the morning, O Lord, you hear my voice; in the morning I lay my requests before you and wait in expectation." (Psalm 5:3)

Chapter 28

Sexuality and Spirituality

IS THERE ANY woman who doesn't enjoy a good love story? Or even a bad one? Many of the great stories from the past have love as their theme. Think David and Bathsheba, Ruth and Boaz, Romeo and Juliet, Lancelot and Guinevere, Anthony and Cleopatra. Think movies such as *Gone with the Wind*, *Casa Blanca*, *Titanic*, *West Side Story*, or even *Shreck*.

There's something in our soul that gravitates toward a love story. And it's all the more magnetic when the story includes romance, intrigue, danger, betrayal, broken hearts—and sex.

As any good romance writer knows, and as any woman who loves a good love story knows, the point is usually not the physical attraction, though that can be powerful. The point is the HEART. Will he get the girl? Will she betray him? Will he break her heart? Will she realize how much he wants her? To what lengths will they go to be together?

There's a truly grand love story going on right now. It's both the oldest and the newest of all love stories. All the other love stories in the world in some way take their themes from this Original Love Story. It has all the elements necessary to rival any of the greatest love stories ever told:

- A heroine who doesn't realize her own beauty or power
- A villain who's determined to imprison her, degrade her beauty, and destroy her power
- A hero who loves her with passion and true, undying love
- Betrayal, intrigue, risk, pain, and death
- A rescue at the last possible moment
- A true Happily Ever After

Doesn't that sound awesome?! And in case you haven't guessed yet, YOU are the heroine!

Why do you think so many of the great love stories picture the heroine's heart being torn between her true lover and an imposter? Isn't it because in the deepest reaches of our hearts we feel the wooing? We feel God's enemy, Satan, pulling at us with forbidden thrills and empty promises of instant gratification. And we feel God wooing us with unselfish love and grace.

Yes, you're the heroine in the story, and it's your heart that's up for grabs. It's your loyalty, allegiance, and love that both the villain and the Hero are after.

And that's where our own sexuality offers such a revealing insight into the Big Story God is writing.

Sexuality at Its Worst, and at Its Best

Think of the worst possible scenarios you've either experienced or know about in relation to a woman's sexuality. You may think of such words as *pain, exploitation, perversion, violence, abuse, molestation, control, ownership, trafficking*, and more. Especially if you've been hurt in this area, the idea of sexuality may leave you feeling dirty, used, discarded, powerless, violated, and betrayed. Feelings such as fear, terror, revulsion, pain, anger, and despair may overwhelm you.

Those are the very same words we could use to describe the kingdom of darkness. God's enemy, Satan, does everything in his power to violate, imprison, deceive, degrade, humiliate, and destroy anyone he can. You see a picture of his true nature in those who throughout history have used sex as a weapon. Armies have used rape to control, capture, and humiliate entire populations. Some husbands and fathers have used it to do the same to their families. Evil people have used it for millennia to make merchandise of other human beings.

Are you sick enough of the idea yet?

Now think of the very best you've experienced, or can possibly imagine, in relation to your sexuality. You may think of words such as *ecstasy, exhilaration, joy, pleasure, comfort, intimacy, security,* and *love*. The absolute best possible sexual experience might leave you feeling special, priceless, cherished, known, safe, satisfied, beautiful, and loved. Time would stand still. During that time you and your lover would feel alone in the universe.

That's the very picture God wants you to have of Him and of your relationship with Him. Those very same words apply in that context. No wonder Paul exclaimed, "No eye has seen, no ear has heard, no mind has conceived what God has prepared for those who love Him" (1 Corinthians 2:9). For now and throughout eternity what God has in mind are intimacy, security, joy, and love between yourself and Him.

Can you glimpse a little more of why God took a chance on creating us as sexual beings? How else could we understand this much of what He wants for us?

The Greatest Love Story

So what about that greatest love story of all? Is it playing out for you as it does in the movies? What about those questions that define the intrigue of a love story?

Will he get the girl? Will she betray him?

In some of the most poignant and heartfelt cries in the Bible God speaks in the voice of a spurned lover:

- "Why should I forgive you? Your children have forsaken me and sworn by gods that are not gods. I supplied all their needs, yet they committed adultery and thronged to the houses of prostitutes." (Jeremiah 5:7)

- "How can I give you up, Ephraim? How can I hand you over, Israel? . . . My heart is changed within me; all my compassion is aroused." (Hosea 11:8)

- "O Jerusalem, Jerusalem, you who kill the prophets and stone those sent to you, how often I have longed to gather your children together, as a hen gathers her chicks under her wings, but you were not willing!" (Luke 13:34)

For some of us, we can say "Yes, He has His girl." We have decided to give our allegiance to the God who created us. We have felt His kiss and chosen to await His arrival to take us home.

And yet you and I HAVE betrayed Him. While waiting for Him we have chosen lesser lovers and allowed our allegiance, in whole or in part, to be directed to them. Whether or not we recognize it, we've broken the heart of our One True Love.

Will he break her heart?

The one thing about Him we know for sure is that He can be trusted. God doesn't always act in ways we can understand or explain, but He IS good. And He has promised "Never will I leave you; never will I forsake you" (Hebrews 13:5).

Yes, our hearts get broken. But not by Him. Remember: the villain is still alive. We're not at the end of the story just yet. As in the movies, the villain tries to make us think it's our True Love who's letting us down. But it isn't. Our rescue has begun, but it isn't finished yet.

Will she realize how much he wants her?

This is the point at which you have a choice right now. You get to write this part of the story. Will you let Satan fool you with instant gratification and lies? Or will you keep returning to your True Love, even when things look dark?

Remember, He wants you regardless of where you've been, where you are now, or how many times you've failed. "Whoever comes to me I will never drive away" (John 6:37).

To what lengths will they go to be together?

For His part, He's already come all the way from heaven to rescue you. But that rescue isn't yet complete. He died to set you free, and He's committed to bringing you back to be His Precious One forever.

Now, today, will you return His love? It's up to you.

Suggested Discussion Questions:

1. *How do the themes in the ideal love story mirror the story of God and His people? The story of God and you?*

2. *"It's your loyalty, allegiance, and love that both the villain and the Hero are after." Do you agree with that statement? Does it help you understand what God wants most from you?*

3. *How does your own experience with sexuality, positive or negative, impact your relationship with God?*

Suggested Action Steps:

1. *Look at your own sexual history. Write a list of words or phrases that describe how you have felt or feel now about this aspect of your life.*

2. *Read your list of words aloud to God in prayer. Then read aloud this this quote from Jesus: "All that the Father gives me will come to me, and whoever comes to me I will never drive away" (John 6:37). Now pause and listen for what Jesus wants to speak in your heart.*

3. *Do you know for certain who has your allegiance, loyalty, and love? Do you need to clarify that with God again? Do so now.*

Scripture to Contemplate or Memorize:

"However, as it is written: 'No eye has seen, no ear has heard, no mind has conceived what God has prepared for those who love him.'" (1 Corinthians 2:9)

Chapter 29

"Unless You Forgive..."

CORRIE TEN BOOM and her sister Betsie were arrested by the Nazis in 1944 in Holland for hiding Jews in their home. The two women were sent to the Ravensbruck concentration camp in Germany, where Betsie died. Corrie was released because of a "clerical error" just days before all of the other women her age in the camp were to be killed.

After the war Corrie became a spokeswoman for the grace of God, often speaking about forgiveness. After one meeting in Germany she was approached by a man who had been one of the camp guards instrumental in her sister Betsie's death. He had become a Christian and came to ask for her forgiveness. She struggled greatly for a moment, awash in feelings of dread and hurt. And then she chose to extend her hand to him. She wrote, "I had never known God's love so intensely as I did then."

For years after the war Corrie maintained rehabilitation centers in Holland for victims of the concentration camps and also for the Dutch collaborators, who were now also being mistreated. But not everyone recovered: "Those who were able to forgive their former enemies were able also to return to the outside world and rebuild their lives, no matter what the physical scars. Those who nursed their bitterness remained invalids. It was as simple and as horrible as that."[1]

If you've been wronged (and who hasn't been?), you may feel as justified as Corrie did in holding a grudge. Someone stole a lot of money from you. Your spouse cheated on you. Someone told horrible lies about you. You were physically, sexually, or emotionally abused. You were purposely passed over in a business deal. A loved one was killed. Your life will never be the same.

There comes a time after every such horrible wrong when you must make a decision. And it's yours alone to make. You have only two choices. Do you:

- Remain hurt, nurse your bitterness, and stay miserable, or
- Do the hard work of forgiveness?

You know Jesus' words: "For if you forgive men when they sin against you, your heavenly Father will also forgive you" (Matthew 6:14). And we've heard a lot about that from preachers. But we should also be hearing more about forgiveness from doctors.

Holding onto bitterness and lack of forgiveness has been associated with many health problems, including immune dysfunction, chronic pain, and even cancer. The research keeps piling up,[2] but the basic message is the same: beyond being bad for your emotions and your soul, an unforgiving attitude hurts your body.

What Is Forgiveness?

Forgiveness is one of the hardest things for many people to do. There's often sweet misery in nursing your wounds. Having been hurt is a wonderful excuse for all kinds of bad behavior. But even though it's hard, forgiveness is both possible and necessary.

Misunderstanding forgiveness has only made it harder for some to experience it, and this has caused even more pain. Here's what forgiveness is, and what it isn't:

Forgiveness is NOT:

- A feeling. A change in your emotional state will come with time, but you don't have to feel different to offer forgiveness. Forgiving feelings follow forgiving actions—sometimes only long afterward.

- Saying "It's OK." It's NOT OK! That's the very reason forgiveness is so necessary. There's no way to make what happened OK. Forgiveness sets you free from the pain of its not being OK.

- Immediate removal of the hurt. You can cry, bleed, and hurt for some time even after offering forgiveness. Bitterness and hate go away with forgiveness, but not necessarily all the pain.

- Allowing yourself to be hurt again. You can forgive and still protect yourself (and others you care about), if necessary, from further harm. Forgiving doesn't mean putting yourself under the control of someone who is likely to hurt you again. The choice of whether or not to continue a relationship is separate from the decision to forgive.

- Assuming that the relationship will be fixed. The relationship with the individual who hurt you MAY be healed, but you can forgive and find freedom whether or not that happens.

Forgiveness IS:

- Difficult! If it were easy, it wouldn't be true forgiveness.

- A choice. Forgiveness begins with an act of your will, not with a feeling.

- A process. It rarely happens in a moment. Sometimes you may need to make the choice to forgive over and over again.

- Personal. No one can tell you when or how to forgive. Sometimes the hardest person to forgive is yourself. If you struggle with this, remember how much God has already forgiven you (Romans 5:8–10).

- Not dependent on the one needing to be forgiven. You can forgive and be free whether or not the other person acknowledges their wrongdoing or receives your forgiveness.

- Godly. You have been forgiven much (Luke 7:47). The forgiveness you offer is nothing more than God's forgiveness passing through your soul.

- Giving up your right to seek revenge and letting God deal with the consequences to the offender (Romans 12:19). Forgiveness is letting go.

How Do You Forgive?

Just because you make the choice to forgive doesn't immediately make the forgiveness take place. The process is more complex and individual than a simple list of steps can fully explore. But here are some important steps:

1. **Acknowledge the hurt.** Don't sugarcoat how bad the wrong was to you and/or to those you care about. Give yourself time to feel the pain.

2. **Express the hurt in some way.** That may be in a journal or diary or in a letter you never mail. It may be to a pastor, a counselor, or a trustworthy friend.

3. **Seek God's perspective.** God hurts when His children hurt. In making my own decision to forgive, it helped me to understand to some small degree how deeply God felt my pain.

4. **Make the decision to forgive.** Don't wait for a feeling. Make the choice to let go of your right to exact revenge for the wrong done to you.

5. **Verbalize forgiveness in prayer.** Pray something like this: "Dear God, I let go of my right to get revenge on (name the person) for (name the wrong). I turn that over to You. I need your help, but I choose to allow

Your forgiveness to work through me in letting this wrong go."

If you can safely do so, you MAY choose to tell the person who wronged you that you're extending them forgiveness. That's a choice only you can make. But you can find the freedom of forgiveness whether or not you do so.

Holding a grudge is like drinking poison and expecting the other person to die.

If you'd rather hold a grudge and take the risk, I can't stop you. But I hope you'll do the hard work of learning to let it go. I'm certain I wouldn't have the life I have now if I hadn't learned how to forgive.

Have you ever met an older person who is bitter and unhappy, with a shriveled-up body and soul? Don't let that happen to you!

Bad stuff happens to all of us—to Corrie Ten Boom, to you, to me. But how long are you going to let that reality control you?

I wish for you the freedom of forgiveness.

Suggested Discussion Questions:

1. *Share an example of forgiveness—in your own life or in that of someone you know or know about.*

2. *"The decision to forgive is separate from the decision of whether or not to continue a relationship." Talk about what that means in your specific context.*

3. *How do you know whether you have truly forgiven someone? Can you forgive without having your feelings change? Why or why not?*

Suggested Action Steps:

1. *Look at your emotional life. Are there wrongs you've experienced about which you're still bitter? Write down a list.*

2. *Read the Scripture verses in this chapter about forgiveness. Using a concordance or other tool, do your own*

search for Bible verses about forgiveness. Let those words rest in your soul.

3. *Dare to make the decision to forgive. Use the prayer in Point 5, above, to verbalize your forgiveness to God.*

Scripture to Contemplate or Memorize:

"Therefore, I tell you, her many sins have been forgiven—for she loved much. But he who has been forgiven little loves little." (Luke 7:47)

Chapter 30

In Love and War: The Action Part of Love

AGNES GONXHA BOJAXHIU was born in 1910 to a devout Catholic family in Albania. When she died in 1997 she was known to the world as Mother Teresa. From 1948 until her death she and her fellow Missionaries of Charity ministered to the sick and dying among the poorest of the poor in Calcutta, India. In her later years she received numerous awards for her work in bringing love to suffering humanity, among them the 1979 Nobel Peace Prize. She left behind over 4,000 Missionaries of Charity Sisters serving in 123 countries around the world.

To many, Mother Teresa is the modern day epitome of Christian love. If nothing else, her life and ministry demonstrate that love isn't a feeling but an action. She showed what it is to see Jesus in "the least of these" (Matthew 25:40; see also James 2:16).

What have YOU done in the name of love? Stayed up all night nursing a sick child—over and over again? Given months, or maybe even years of your life as caregiver to a sick parent or spouse? Stuck by someone as they struggled with a mental illness or an addiction? Defied conventional wisdom and married someone others thought wouldn't be good for you?

It isn't that every one of these actions is in itself always good or wise: it's the fact that we do them! Love has gotten a cheap reputation because of its inglorious imitators, such as Lust, Greed, Control, and Dependency. But love is still the most powerful force ever granted by God to us human beings. It makes us risk things we'd never risk for any other reason, find energy we didn't realize we had, and go beyond ourselves over and over again.

And that makes it gloriously dangerous.

What Is a True Picture of Love?

What picture comes to mind when you think of love?

- A mother tenderly nurturing her baby?
- A young man on one knee asking his sweetheart for her hand?
- Feelings of well-being while in your loved one's embrace?
- Jesus holding out His hand, saying "I forgive you"?

Yes, all of those images depict much about love. But there's something relatively superficial about them. Instead, think of the picture of love in the classic fairy tale formula in which the fair maiden is held captive by someone or something evil. The dashing young suitor must wage war against dragons or demons or hell itself to rescue her, all in the name of love. The picture of love that resonates most within us is also a picture of war!

You may not have ever felt that someone loved you enough to fight for you. But part of you knows this aspect of love. A loving parent would take on anyone who would try to harm their child. A loving friend would be willing to risk harm to help the one they cared about. A loving husband would shoulder the weight of the world to provide for and protect his wife and family.

What does love mean to God? He saw the object of His love—you—in trouble. He saw you broken, sick, and alienated in your messed up, sinful world, held captive by His enemy and doomed. But He didn't just look on in pity; He took action. He came down from heaven in the person of Jesus, at great cost to Himself, and fought hell itself to rescue you and win your heart.

And then He works His wonderful "magic" in you to change you into the glorious person He created you to be, and to create a truly "happily ever after" future for you. He's gone to war for you against His enemy (and yours), and He has won.

It's a picture of love . . . and war.

Going to War for Love

But what about you? What are YOU doing in the name of love? Is there anyone or anything you care about enough to DO something about? What is it that's putting the object(s) of your love in danger? What are you doing about that?

Such action starts at home. If you're married, remember that your spouse isn't your enemy. (There are exceptions. If you're concerned that your spouse is or may be your enemy, review chapter 22.) But there are things that are putting your spouse is danger. They could be anxiety, fear, overwork, other people's opinions, negative self-talk, etc. How are you helping support your spouse in overcoming those dangers?

If you're a parent, you may understand this aspect of parental love quite well. The culture at large, well-meaning friends, and God's enemy all have plans for your children. Part of your job as a parent is to wage war against any dangers and then to help your children develop their own strength to stand against them.

And then there's the larger picture. Many people struggle with the idea of a calling or purpose. Beyond your family, what has God asked you to do? How can you know? What are you supposed to be doing in this life?

Here's another question that may help you find the answer:

What breaks your heart? Over whose pain do you cry? Whose joy do you celebrate?

When you recognize whose pain you feel, you've identified the problem God has put you on this Earth to help fix. Your own heartbreak is likely to be the very quality in you God uses to bring healing and blessings to others.

If you know the pain of addiction and feel the heartbreak of those struggling to break free, you know the kind of people you can speak to. If children dying from disease because of the lack of clean water in various areas of the world keeps you awake, you know the kind of charity or mission to get involved with. If battered women, human trafficking victims, young adults who don't know how to read, homeless families, or those struggling with depression get under your skin, you know whom God wants you to help.

Perhaps your heart is broken by those affected by domestic violence, mental illness, poverty, hunger, gambling, pornography, or addiction. Perhaps it's lonely seniors, sick children, returning military personnel, prisoners or their families, or those fighting a particular illness. The people on your heart may be in your own neighborhood or on the other side of the globe.

If there's any love in your heart, it demands action.

And as far as your love for God, that demands action too. Jesus said so: "If you love me, you will obey what I command" (John 14:15). Loving God means doing what He says, letting Him change your whole being, and following through on the mission He's sending you to do.

So why not let your love stir your heart enough to go to war. Make sure you remember that the one(s) you love aren't the enemy. You're fighting against whomever or whatever is putting them in danger.

So think about it. What breaks your heart?

Now what are you going to do about it?

Suggested Discussion Questions:

1. *What example or picture of love means the most to you? Why?*

2. *What actions have you taken based on your love? Have you ever fought to protect someone you cared about, or to make others' lives better?*

3. *Have you experienced God in some way using your brokenness to bless others? Talk about what that's been like.*

Suggested Action Steps:

1. *Look at the people closest to you. How can your love show itself in action for their benefit?*

2. *Whose pain has your experience allowed you to feel? Can you see how God is using your experience to bless others who are feeling that pain now?*

3. *Spend some time in prayer, talking with God about how your love can show itself in action in a larger way.*

Scripture to Contemplate or Memorize:

"The King will reply, 'I tell you the truth, whatever you did for one of the least of these brothers of mine, you did for me.'" (Matthew 25:40)

Chapter 31

What God Will NOT Do for You

PAULA WAS VISITING a new church this weekend. Perhaps this time she would find the answer she was looking for. The last church she'd tried had been nice enough, and the pastor had often preached about the wonderful things God would do for her. But Paula's marriage was still in shambles, her diabetes was out of control, and the debt collectors were still calling. It was hard for her to avoid becoming discouraged.

Paula had high hopes for this new church. A friend had told her about how the pastor seemed to know exactly what she needed every time she asked for prayer. Paula determined to ask him to pray for her at her first opportunity. Perhaps this time God would hear and help her with her problems.

If God cares about Paula's marriage, her diabetes, and her financial problems, why doesn't He do something about them? Why doesn't He heal her of diabetes, bring her the winning lottery ticket, and make her husband stop drinking? She's asked Him to do all these things. Doesn't He hear her prayers?

Ask most Christians if there's anything God can't do, and they'll tell you NO. "For nothing is impossible with God" (Luke 1:37). The Bible tells us so!

Then why do so many Christians struggle with such problems as pornography, obesity, debt, marriage problems, addiction, and more? Why doesn't a God who loves and cares and can do anything fix these problems for those who ask Him?

Perhaps you're beginning to see a problem with this way of thinking. It may even be a little dangerous to attempt an answer to such big questions. We live in a complicated, sinful world, and we can never begin to resolve every Why? question this side of heaven. But here's an important truth:

> *Try to take charge of that which is in God's hands, and you'll become frustrated and anxious. Neglect to take charge of what God has placed in YOUR hands, and you'll become depressed and ineffective.*

You mean to say that God isn't in charge of everything?

Yes, in the ultimate sense God IS in charge. "He's got you and me, sister, in His hands. He's got the whole world in His hands."

But there are some extremely important things God has placed under YOUR control. And He won't grab those things out of your hands to do for you what's in your power to do for yourself.

Here are a few things God won't do for you. God won't:

- Take the fork out of your hand if you need to lose weight.
- Hide your credit cards if you need to get out of debt.
- "Beam you" home from work if you need to spend more time with your husband and children.
- Chain you to the bedpost if you need to pray.

Those may sound like drastic examples, but the point is important. God loves doing wonderfully good things for you as His child. But He won't remove your ability to choose, to act, and to experience the results of your choices and actions.

Where YOU Are in Charge

God has given you executive authority over your life and a significant part of His kingdom. He created humankind to govern, to rule over many aspects of this Earth (see Genesis 1:26). He calls us to be kings and priests with delegated authority under the supreme King and Priest, Christ Jesus (Revelation 1:6). God expects you to govern the part of His kingdom He has put within your care, and He has fitted you to do so.

How freeing it is when you own that idea! You get to decide, under God, so much more than you realize. You get to experience the fulfillment of wrestling with the decisions and seeing the fruit of your labor. You can't control everything, but your choices do have consequences. Big ones.

Here are some things over which God has put you in charge:

1. **Your lifestyle.** You get to decide what you eat, how you care for your body, when and how you rest, what you do or don't put into your body, how you present yourself in terms of your physical appearance, and more.

2. **Your time.** He has given each of us 168 hours a week. Nobody has any more than you do. You get to choose how you spend that time—complaining and wasting it or learning, enjoying, and helping others.

3. **Your money.** Yes, YOU get to choose how much money to make, how hard to work in making it, how much to give and to whom, what to spend it on, and how to invest or save it.

4. **Your attitude.** Good and bad things happen to each of us, and each of us responds differently. YOU get to choose whether to be angry, depressed, courageous, kind, generous, bitter, or loving.

5. **Who you spend time with.** Who said you have to spend your time around people who make you miserable? You get to choose to spend your time with people who are uplifting, who appreciate what you can give, or whom you can help.

6. **What you give, and to whom you give it.** All of us give: financial or material goods, attention, love, time. You're in charge of what flows from your life to others.

7. **Your family.** No, you can't control anyone else. But you get to choose what impact your life has on the people closest to you. God put them in your life for you to nurture, love, encourage, and help in their life and spiritual journey.

8. **Your life legacy.** What will be left after you're gone? You get to choose the work you do and how your life and efforts impact others for the future. You can choose to leave the world a better place.

9. **What others believe about God.** If you call yourself a Christian, YOU are the most effective advertisement for God to those who don't know Him. You can choose the impression others have of God based on what they see and hear from you.

10. **Your worship.** Each one of us worships someone or something—money, fame, comfort, or others' opinions. God hopes you'll worship Him! But He won't force you. That's your choice.

There are many things God has promised to do for you. And He's eager to fulfill those promises.

But He also believes in and respects you enough to give you a great deal of free will and responsibility.

God provides you with so much, including second chances. And third chances. And wisdom and courage and opportunities and love and forgiveness and hope and a future and His presence.

Now, what are you going to do about the things He's placed under your care? You can't fix or control everything. But what are you doing about those things you CAN change?

In the next chapter we'll talk more about what it looks like to cooperate in working together with God. And it's very good news.

Suggested Discussion Questions:

1. *Can you think of other things God will NOT do for you? Things He has placed under YOUR care?*

2. *What's your emotional response to the reality that there are some things God won't do on your behalf? Angry? Frustrated? Excited? Liberated? Talk about your response.*

3. *In what area of life that God has left under your care have you not been doing very well? What could you do to better take charge of that area?*

Suggested Action Steps:

1. *Write down a list of the things you most often pray for.*

2. *Look over your list for any areas God has left in your control. Identify an action step you can take this week to help answer your own prayer.*

3. *Pray the Serenity Prayer: "God, grant me the serenity to accept the things I cannot change, the courage to change the things I can, and the wisdom to know the difference."*

Scripture to Contemplate or Memorize:

"You have made them to be a kingdom and priests to serve our God, and they will reign on the earth." (Revelation 5:10)

Chapter 32

"God, Help Me!"
Working Together with God

SOMETHING DIDN'T MAKE sense to Dr. Kenneth Pargament. As a clinical psychologist, he was fascinated by how his clients faced difficult issues involving meaning, isolation, loss, tragedy, and death. Many of his clients spoke of how important their faith was at such times. Faith seemed to be a powerful resource that helped them come through those difficulties while maintaining a high degree of mental and physical health.

Other clients seemed to fare much worse. Some faced challenges no more impressive than his "healthy" clients, but their spiritual beliefs and practices seemed to only add to their suffering. While they talked about God often, their challenges seemed to leave them "used up" physically, mentally, and spiritually.

What made the difference? What was it about the spiritual life of some people that seemed to help them weather tough stuff and come out healthier? And what was it about the spiritual life of others that was detrimental to their long-term well-being? What made spirituality "work" for some and not for others?

Dr. Pargament set out to find the answers, and 40 years later his work has become a significant part of the expanding research on spirituality and health. He has evaluated thousands of people in many settings: mid-western church members, survivors of the Oklahoma City bombing, cancer and heart disease patients, seniors with serious health problems, mental health patients, and more.

Dr. Pargament's summary is worth noting again:

> *Some forms of religion are more helpful than others. A religion that is internalized, intrinsically motivated, and built on a belief in a greater meaning in life, a secure relationship with God, and a sense of spiritual connectedness with others has positive implications for well-being. Conversely, a religion that is imposed, unexamined, and reflective of a tenuous relationship with God and the world bodes poorly for well-being.*[1]

In interviewing thousands of people, Dr. Pargament found that people generally fall into one of three categories in terms of how they use their spirituality when they face difficulties. One group he described as "self-directing." People within this group may believe in God, but for all practical purposes they see themselves as responsible for solving their own problems. A second group he called "deferring." These individuals generally look to God to solve their problems and don't take any significant action on their own.

A third group he called "collaborative." These individuals see themselves as actively working together with God in dealing with their problems. Their spirituality tends to be founded on "an intimate personal interactive relationship with God."[2]

People respond uniquely to the problems they encounter. But in general, the research demonstrated that people who face their problems from a "collaborative" standpoint—working together with God—generally come through challenges with better mental and physical health and a stronger spirituality.

Working with God

The Bible talks about the same principle. Paul said, "Continue to work out your salvation with fear and trembling, for it is God who works in you to will and to act according to his good purpose" (Philippians 2:12,13).

So there are things God does. And there are things you do. Remember the little girls trying to get to school on time (chapter 1)? We're talking about running while you pray. It's a both/and proposition. You do your part and trust God to do His.

So how does that work? Here's what that might look like in a few specific situations.

If you're physically sick or unhealthy:

Your job:

- Learn all you can about your illness or dysfunction.
- Make any physical lifestyle changes you need to make.
- Get appropriate professional help (physician, nutritionist, psychologist, etc.).
- Diligently follow any treatment plans available to help you get well.
- Pray for healing, and ask others to pray for you.

God's job:

- Direct you to the most appropriate help.
- Provide you wisdom and strength to make any necessary lifestyle changes.
- Provide you courage to persevere when the going gets tough.
- Provide comfort and love all the time.
- Provide healing—in His timing and way.

If you're out of work and looking for a job:

Your job:

- Be wise and diligent in conserving your material resources.
- Be wise and diligent in looking for or creating a job.

- Network with anyone and everyone you can.
- Work hard at developing any skills necessary to be financially productive, including a right attitude.
- Pray—for God to bring you resources, ideas, and connections, as well as for income.

God's job:

- Provide insight and ideas regarding sources of income.
- Bring helpful people or resources into your life.
- Provide courage and wisdom if you need to create rather than find a job.
- Remind you that you aren't defined by your income but by your standing as His child.

If you're struggling in a bad marriage:

Your job:

- Honestly evaluate your own attitudes and behavior.
- Work diligently on such skills as communication, forgiveness, patience, and love.
- Allow God to change anything in you that's contributing to the dysfunction.
- Take full advantage of any resources or help to improve your marriage.
- Pray—for yourself, for your spouse, and for your marriage.

God's job:

- Soften and transform your heart and life to help you be a good partner.
- Work in your spouse's life to do the same.
- Forgive you and your spouse for past wrongs.

- Provide wisdom, courage, strength, and resources to help your marriage grow.

Are you getting an idea of how this works?

Sometimes there are situations in which there's nothing within our power that will change anything. The good news is that God still has those situations in His hands. But most of the time there's a lot we can do to cooperate with Him. That's where praying for "wisdom to know the difference" is so important.

No, God won't take the fork out of your hand, vaporize your credit cards, or chain you to the bedpost to pray.

But He WILL:

- Take control of any area of your life you'll allow Him to.
- Be there for you, whether or not you're aware of it.
- Forgive you when you ask.
- Provide a ready supply of courage, wisdom, resources, wisdom, and love.

Aren't you glad you don't have to do it all on your own?

And aren't you also glad for the ways in which you can cooperate with God for your own benefit and for the benefit of others around you?

Suggested Discussion Questions:

1. *Which of Dr. Pargament's three coping styles do you use most of the time —self-directing, deferring, or collaborative? Give an example of how your usual strategy has worked for you.*

2. *Think of a serious problem you or someone you know is facing. What might be God's part? What might be your part in dealing with the issue?*

3. *What Bible character can you think of who demonstrates the idea of cooperating with God?*

Suggested Action Steps:

1. Look at the list of things you often pray for from the last chapter. As you think about your prayers, what coping style do you think they display?

2. Pick one item from your list. Write down three things you know God will do in that area for you, and three things you believe are your responsibility.

3. Keep praying the Serenity Prayer: "God, grant me the serenity to accept the things I cannot change, the courage to change the things I can, and the wisdom to know the difference. Amen."

Scripture to Contemplate or Memorize:

"Therefore, my dear friends, as you have always obeyed—not only in my presence, but now much more in my absence—continue to work out your salvation with fear and trembling, for it is God who works in you to will and to act according to his good purpose." (Philippians 2:12,13)

Chapter 33

What Is Healthy Spirituality?

SANDRA HAS TRIED. She really has! She's been reading her Bible and knows God has a plan for her. But the church thing has been difficult. Over the past several years she has joined several different churches in her town, one after another. Each time she's been overjoyed at connecting with the family of God and felt welcomed by the people with whom she connected.

But then something happens. She told me, "Once I join, I feel like the people in the church are just watching me, waiting for me to mess up. I feel like I have to prove myself, and if I can't make the grade I'm treated as an outcast."

Sandra isn't sure she can try church again. She feels bruised and beaten emotionally and spiritually at the hands of other Christians.

Is any of this her fault? Should she have done things differently? I suppose that's possible. But what's most important is that one of God's children has been wounded.

I hope God breaks through to Sandra at some point. I hope she comes to realize that true followers of Jesus don't beat up other people! The Christian life is challenging. God calls us to a higher plane of living than we ever dreamed possible. But spiritual abuse isn't of God.

Unhealthy spirituality can be toxic—to your mental well-being, your physical health, and your relationship with God.

But how do you know if you're experiencing one of these distortions of true Christianity? Here are four dangerous spiritual viruses to watch out for:

1. Cheap Grace

Jesus offers us grace—overwhelming, undeserved, mind-blowing grace. And we all need that grace desperately. The good news is that no matter how low we've fallen, God's grace is there to forgive and restore. We can't do anything to earn that grace; it's completely free. That's the gospel.

But that isn't the end of the message of the gospel. The free gift of grace doesn't deal only with our past; it also deals with our future. God loves you just the way you are, but He loves you too much to leave you that way.

God loves us enough to change us from the broken, angry, selfish, immature, violent, hate-filled, miserable, or addicted people we are when He finds us. He sets about transforming us into the glorious, courageous, loving, joyous, mature members of His kingdom He knows we can be. Cheap grace, on the other hand, stops at the beginning and ignores both the reality and the necessity of the transforming power of God's grace (Romans 6:15).

That transformation process may take much longer than you wish, but God won't stop if you don't. Let Him change you.

2. Rigid External Perfectionism

The standard God sets is high. The problem comes when people demand a human brand of perfection, both of themselves and of others. As a result such people often become mean-spirited and angry, typically overlooking the inner aspects of character God prizes most. They develop a hierarchy of sins, and heaven help you if you mess up in one of the "bigger" sin categories! Too often their own efforts to live perfectly break down, and some secret sin becomes exposed.

Jesus called people to a completely different type of life from that which religion promotes. Religious rituals mean very little when held up against more important matters, such as mercy, justice, and faith (Mathew 23:23). Godly outward behavior must flow from a transformed inner heart. White-knuckling it doesn't work very long anyway.

Perfectionism will leave us bitter, frustrated, or proud. God's grace is the only remedy for perfectionism—or, for that matter, for any other spiritual dysfunction. Let Him change you—from the inside out.

3. Lack of Responsibility

Perhaps you know someone who has just one answer to every problem: "Pray about it." That's good, right? The problem comes when we behave like the first of the two little girls rushing to get to school. We stop running when we should be both praying and running.

God does do amazing, miraculous things. But as we talked about in chapter 31, there are some things God won't do *for* you. It's right that we remember and celebrate what God has promised, but that doesn't negate our own responsibility to follow through with obedience to what He asks of us.

Jesus offered a helpful picture of our responsibility in the story of the man who built his house on the rock: "Everyone who hears these words of mine and puts them into practice" will have a life that storms cannot destroy (see Matthew 7:24–27). A spirituality that denies our personal responsibility to act is only foolish.

Our prayers may often be answered by a change in our own understanding, our own heart, or our own behavior. Welcome that aspect of God's intervention in your life just as much as you do His instantaneous miracles.

4. Playing Holy Spirit

If you've given God permission to work in you, at some point you'll come to understand His ways of communicating to you through His Holy Spirit. This becomes a very precious and intimate part of your relationship with Him.

But it's possible to confuse God's voice with that of other people, or even of the enemy. There are those who claim to speak for God when they're speaking out of their own imagination, or worse. God doesn't look kindly on that behavior (Jeremiah 14:14).

When religious people use God-talk to manipulate and control you, this is a sign of distorted, toxic spirituality. You dare not give any human being the place in your soul that only God should hold through His Holy Spirit. If you sense leaders trying to put themselves in God's place in your life, seek God's guidance and move on.

Healthy Spirituality:

If that's toxic religion, what is healthy spirituality? Those distortions make the real thing so much more appealing. Healthy spirituality involves at least these elements:

- A growing relationship with a loving God
- Experiencing God's grace and forgiveness for the past
- Experiencing God's transforming power in becoming ever more like Jesus
- Relationships with other Christians that are characterized by humility, accountability, and love

Will Sandra recover from the religious bruising she has experienced? God's grace is certainly big enough for that to happen. And the really good news: none of these spiritual viruses need result in a terminal illness. God has the antidote ready for you.

We'll talk a little more in the next chapter about the results of healthy spirituality.

Suggested Discussion Questions:

1. *What examples of toxic religion have you seen?*
2. *How do you know when distorted Christianity is in play? What role does Scripture, intuition, or experience play in helping you understand this?*
3. *Have you been guilty yourself of any distorted or toxic religion?*

Suggested Action Steps:

1. *On a scale of 1 to 5, how "infected" would you say you are with the four spiritual viruses listed above (Cheap Grace,*

Rigid Perfectionism, Lack of Responsibility, and Playing Holy Spirit)? Make a note of your thoughts.

2. *Thoughtfully read the Scriptures listed in the four sections of this chapter.*

3. *Each day this week spend 15 minutes quietly in God's presence. Ask Him to speak to you about any spiritual healing you may need.*

Scripture to Contemplate or Memorize:

"Therefore, there is now no condemnation for those who are in Christ Jesus, because through Christ Jesus the law of the Spirit of life set me free from the law of sin and death." (Romans 8:1,2)

Chapter 34

How to Know If Your Faith Is Working

IF YOU WERE to walk into the home where our oldest grandson lives, you'd see a wall with lots of pencil marks on it. Beside each mark Mommy or Daddy has written a date. Andrew loves to look at the wall to see how much taller he has become every few months. And he loves to point out that fact to his proud grandparents as well.

Looking back at how much I'd grown was one of the most encouraging things to me during the early part of my Christian walk. God is the only One whose evaluation ultimately matters. But He has told us a lot about how much He wants us to grow, and what that looks like.

So how about you? Where are your "marks on the wall"?

You go to church—or don't. You have a Bible on the table and read it—sometimes. You pray—more than most, but not as much as some. Your coworkers know you're a Christian and don't seem to care too much. You don't look or sound anything like Sally SuperChristian, but that's just not your personality. You believe God is real, but there are moments when you struggle with doubts about certain things.

Do any of those things really matter? If you're certain of Jesus as your Savior, what kind of difference should that be making in your life now? Do you have to be "super-Christian" to be successful?

When it comes to our relationship with God, checklists can be a little dangerous. He deals with each of us individually, and sometimes in very unique ways. But a spiritual checkup can help you put some "marks on the wall."

Here are a few evaluation points to check:

1. **Are godly characteristics showing up in your life?** Qualities like truthfulness, courage, kindness, honesty, forgiveness, joy, peace, and love (Galatians 5:22,23). These aren't characteristics you can develop by trying harder. They only develop as God works His transforming grace in your soul. If they're showing up in your character, you know He's at work. That's why they're called "fruit."

2. **Are people around you being impacted in a positive way?** It starts with your family; how do they respond when you're around? What about the people around you at work, at church, at school, or on social media? If people who are in trouble or who want to grow themselves are being drawn to you, this may be an indication that God is working through you (2 Corinthians 2:15,16).

3. **Are your sins under control?** That's a tricky one. You certainly can't white-knuckle it and "control" your sins. God's forgiveness is real, and His grace covers you. But as you proceed through the Christian life you shouldn't remain the same. God's work in transforming your heart should increasingly show up in your outward behavior (Romans 6:12–14). If it isn't, something's wrong.

4. **Is your reason for living bigger than yourself?** You can't often see the whole picture of what God wants to do in and through your life. But the longer you know Him, the better you understand His purpose for you,

even if that understanding is imperfect. And that purpose is always larger than just your own comfort. Are your energies being given, in some way, to the advance of His kingdom?

5. **Is your relationship with God stronger now that when you began?** The longer you know God, the stronger your bond with Him should become. You continuously come to know Him better, hear Him better, and love Him more.

Notice that there's nothing on this list about emotions, or church work, or religious activity. And this isn't about a straight line; the Christian life has seasons that may be harder or easier. Just because you don't FEEL better doesn't mean God isn't working in your life.

And how about spiritual maturity? What goal are we after?

What Spiritual Maturity Is NOT

You know people who are emotionally and spiritually children, even though they may have lived already for many years. You know the retired grandmother whom no one wants to be around. She's always complaining about the terrible things life has done to her. Her health is poor. She's bitter and lonely. If you try to offer help, it's never enough. Even her physical body appears shriveled and sad. She's always unhappy, always demanding help, and then criticizing anyone trying to offer that help.

Or there's the middle-aged church deacon who has a spiritual answer for everything. His kids left home at the first opportunity; they couldn't take the micromanagement and constant put-downs any longer. His wife has either deteriorated into a doormat or has left him. He has quoted the same Bible verses for 30 years, often to point out how someone else is failing to follow a scriptural mandate. And yet his personal life is filled with sexual indiscretions, financial cheating, and broken hearts.

Those examples demonstrate what can happen if we focus only on outward religious activity, without ever allowing God to grow us up on the inside. A lack of such internal spiritual maturity is one reason even Christian leaders too often fall. We learn in the Bible that even Jesus had to go through a maturing process, both in body and in spirit (Luke 2:25; Hebrews 5:8).

What Spiritual Maturity IS

So what does a spiritually mature person look like? Where is God working to take you?

Someone who is spiritually mature wouldn't look like a Pharisee. Or a Judas. Or a "doubting Thomas." Legalistic, self-righteous, frightened, anxious, withdrawn, proud, or angry wouldn't fit. Spiritual maturity would, of course, look a lot like Jesus.

Here are some qualities spiritual maturity would include:

- **Strength and courage:** not easily swayed by others' opinions, reasonably confident in your own relationship with God (2 Timothy 1:12)

- **Kind and generous:** looking out more for the needs of others than for your own, freely giving whatever you have to give (Matthew 10:8)

- **Aware of your own weaknesses:** conscious of your own humanity and willing to allow God and others to bring you correction when it's needed (Psalm 139:23,24)

- **Flexible emotionally:** able to weep with those who weep and rejoice with those who rejoice, to express all human emotions when appropriate (Romans 12:15)

- **Response to trouble:** responding with honesty, willing to bring the big questions to God Himself and to accept help from others (Psalm 121:1)

- **Living with integrity:** doing what you say and saying what you do, without any hidden agenda or skeletons in the closet (2 Corinthians 4:2)

If you knew someone like that, wouldn't you enjoy being around them?

We all have a lot of growing to do. Look at this picture of spiritual maturity, put some marks on your own wall, and rejoice at how far God has grown you.

At the same time notice areas in which God may still be working to grow you more. The good news is that there's no time limit on this test; He'll keep working on you as long as you'll let Him.

Suggested Discussion Questions:

1. *What examples of spiritual immaturity can you describe? Think about outward behaviors that demonstrate internal immaturity.*

2. *What examples of spiritual maturity can you describe? What characteristics demonstrate that maturity?*

3. *Describe some "marks on your wall"—some positive changes in your life because you're a follower of Jesus.*

Suggested Action Steps:

1. *If you haven't already, consider starting a journal for the purpose of recording the good things God has done in your life.*

2. *Look back at what your life was like before Jesus, and then consider what your life is like now. Do something to celebrate your growth: write song lyrics or a poem, tell a friend, shout it from a hilltop.*

3. *Which aspect of spiritual maturity do you believe God is working hardest to grow in you right now? Is there anything you can do to cooperate with Him in this area?*

Scripture to Contemplate or Memorize:

"But the fruit of the Spirit is love, joy, peace, patience, kindness, goodness, faithfulness, gentleness and self-control. Against such things there is no law." (Galatians 5:22,23)

Chapter 35

"I Am the God Who Heals You"

I HAVE WRITTEN many prescriptions, performed surgeries, and helped people make healthy lifestyle changes. Often those people get better. Sometimes they don't.

I have prayed for people as a friend, as a physician, and as a minister. Some of those people have told me those prayers were answered. At other times they weren't.

One friend told me that after I prayed for her she was able to sleep through the night for the first time after years of insomnia.

Another woman told me that a genetic blood disorder she'd had since birth disappeared after we prayed for her. For years she had needed phlebotomy every month. But no more.

After speaking at a church service I prayed for a couple struggling with infertility. One year later they welcomed a baby into their home.

Were these people healed? They will tell you Yes. I could tell you many more stories of healing—from physical problems, emotional distress, relationship issues, and more.

But there's also the man I knew who cared for his wife with severe multiple sclerosis, giving her the best medical treatment possible and having many people pray for her. She continued to deteriorate and eventually died.

There's my classmate, a former missionary, who buried his wife shortly before our graduation, after years of her suffering with cancer.

Does God heal today? Why sometimes and not at other times?

The Christian church has a long tradition of caring for the sick and praying for their healing. Many see this as continuing the healing ministry of Jesus. Some branches of the Christian church see God actively healing in the world today and see the church's ministry as inclusive of healing the sick (James 5:15). Other branches of the church teach that such divine healing isn't for today. But even they acknowledge that God CAN heal and that on rare and "special" occasions He still does.

I have both seen and experienced God's healing power. And I've seen some people respond with faith and resilience even though their physical body wasn't healed. I have also seen the trauma, frustration, and despair some people feel when they don't experience the healing they desire and pray for.

If you believe in supernatural healing, you've probably seen or experienced God's healing power personally. If you don't, it probably isn't because of some settled theological belief but because you haven't seen or personally experienced God's healing power. I say this because the theological controversy over divine healing doesn't usually answer the pointed questions that people who need healing are actually asking.

So instead, let's talk about you.

Do You Need Healing?

Right now, think about one thing you'd like God to do for you. Forget for a moment such questions as "Do I deserve it?" "Is that too big, or too small, to ask Him for?" or "Will He do it?" If you could ask God for anything, anything at all, and you KNEW He would do it for you, what would you ask for?

That's the kind of question Jesus often asked. For example, He asked the man lying beside the Pool of Bethesda, "Do you want to get well?" (John 5:6)

The man to whom Jesus addressed that question had been lying there for 38 years. Wouldn't it be obvious that he would want to get well?

What if Jesus were to ask you that question today? Do YOU want to get well?

If you need physical healing, you might say "Of course I want to get well! I want my pain to be gone. I don't want to take this medication anymore. I don't want to have to go to the doctor anymore."

But think of all it would mean for you if you did get well.

- You couldn't use your pain or sickness as an excuse for bad behavior any longer.

- You might have to go back to work, with all that struggle and stress.

- You'd have to acknowledge that God does heal and tell others about it.

- You might be responsible for resources, such as time, strength, and money, you didn't have before.

- You might have to change some bad habits with which you've grown comfortable.

The God we serve has a lot to say about healing. Throughout the Old Testament God presents Himself as the Source of healing (Exodus 15:26; Psalm 102:2,3).

Then Jesus comes upon the scene, and a flood of healing follows everywhere He goes (Matthew 8:16; Luke 6:19). Some of the people Jesus healed were suffering the results of their own sin. Others were enduring pain and sickness completely unrelated to any specific sin. Jesus wasn't nearly as concerned about where the sickness came from as He was about relieving suffering.

Jesus had and has only one attitude toward sickness: **He's against it!**

What Healing Looks Like

In this sinful world we all get sick, sometimes due to our own behavior, sometimes through no fault of our own. God wants us well. So can we do anything about getting healed?

God's goal in our healing is much broader than we usually realize. He's after our complete healing, which includes not only our physical body but also our mind and emotions, our relationships, and our innermost heart and spirit.

Think again of Samantha, who struggles with infertility and pelvic pain. Intimacy with her husband is difficult. She also struggles with guilt after leaving an abusive home at her first opportunity and spending her teen years in numerous sexual relationships. Now she feels that God is punishing her, and she can't believe she'll ever have a happy life, experience a good marriage, or be a mother. Samantha needs more than a pregnancy and relief from pain. She needs to feel God's forgiveness and love. She needs to experience love from her husband and a sense of wholeness in her heart. When she does, she may feel healed, whether or not she becomes a mother.

When we have a fuller understanding of what God is trying to do, we can cooperate with Him better. Yes, He wants you to be physically well. But He wants much more for you as well. He wants the complete redemption of every part of your being.

Why don't more people experience real and lasting healing from God? Some reasons we may only partially understand: these include lack of forgiveness, rebellion and sin, lack of obedience, and spiritual warfare. And some healing happens gradually over time. But often we just don't know the answer.

For my part, I'm going to continue writing prescriptions, doing surgery, praying for people, and trusting God to bring healing wherever possible.

And you? Here's what to do once you answer God's question "What do you want Me to do for you?"

1. **Ask Him.** Pray for healing. Ask others to pray for you. God loves to give good things to His children.

2. **Trust Him.** He loves you. Truly, He does! He's big enough, and good enough, to trust.

3. **Cooperate with Him.** Wherever you can, take action in the direction of your healing. God may use that as a means to bring you the very thing your heart desires.

Remember, God calls Himself "The God Who Heals You" (Exodus 15:26). And He doesn't change.

Suggested Discussion Questions:

1. *Since God says "I am the God who heals you," why do you think more people don't experience healing today?*

2. *What would it look like to be completely healed?*

3. *Have you prayed for divine healing, for yourself or for someone else? What happened?*

Suggested Action Steps:

1. *Write down the answer to God's question to you, "What do you want Me to do for you?" Make it personal and specific.*

2. *List at least three things you can do to cooperate with God in your healing: some lifestyle change, getting professional help, working on a negative attitude, etc.*

3. *If you haven't already done so, ask someone with faith, someone you respect, to pray with you for your healing, or whatever it is you want from God.*

Scripture to Contemplate or Memorize:

"He said, 'If you listen carefully to the voice of the Lord your God and do what is right in his eyes, if you pay attention to his commands and keep all his decrees, I will not bring on you any of the diseases I brought on the Egyptians, for I am the Lord, who heals you.'" (Exodus 15:26)

Chapter 36

Far into the Future: Eternal Medicine

BRONNIE WARE WORKED for several years as a palliative nurse caring for people during their final weeks of life. She recorded her observations in the best-selling memoir *The Top Five Regrets of the Dying*.[1] The Number 1 regret: "I wish I'd had the courage to live a life true to myself, not the life others expected of me." Other top regrets include "I wish I hadn't worked so hard" and "I wish that I had let myself be happier."

Knowing that one has only days or weeks to live seems to change a person's perspective, to provide a clarity and wisdom often lacking in the busyness of life. Moses prayed, "Teach us to number our days" (Psalm 90:12). It may be difficult to fully recognize the forever consequences of our day-to-day decisions, actions, and attitudes. One relationship neglected, one bad habit tolerated, one opportunity not taken, and all you're left with are regrets.

One of the saddest things one can ask at the end of life is "What might have been?!"

Whatever your age, here are some regrets you don't want to carry into death:

1. **Missed time with loved ones.** It takes time to nurture relationships with the people who are most important to you. Your children are small only once. After your parents depart, your time with them is gone forever. Missed opportunities to spend time with your spouse can never be retrieved. Treasure the people close to you while you can. People are truly a once-in-a-lifetime opportunity.

2. **Neglecting your health.** Eating right, exercising, getting appropriate rest, resisting bad habits—who has time for any of that? But once your health is gone, it may not be possible to completely get it back. Value yourself and your loved ones enough to live a healthy life now. As a physician, I see this regret far too often.

3. **Avoidance of risk-taking.** Perhaps it's a trip you'd love to take, an entrepreneurial endeavor you'd love to try, an education you wish you had, or a cause in which you strongly believe. One day it really may be too late. Something has been implanted within you that the world, and the kingdom of God, desperately needs. Sure, it may be risky, but will you regret not having gone for it?

4. **Living someone else's life.** Parents, teachers, bosses, the church, society—there are plenty of people who will gladly tell you what to think and how to live . . . if you let them. But no one else will be looking back at YOUR life with regrets; it will only be you. Live with honesty and integrity, true to the qualities God has built into YOU. God is the only Audience you need truly care about.

5. **Forgetting forever.** Do you know where you'll spend eternity? That's a very, very long time! Make sure things are right between you and God. He promised that if you trust Him He'll take care of your tomorrows—forever.

If you feel a twinge in your heart when you think about forever, don't ignore it. That's the most important symptom of all. God wants so much for you—both here and for eternity. It's common to have some doubts, but I encourage you to make sure things are settled between you and Him.

What you do now will determine whether or not you'll look back at your life with regrets. Don't let that happen to you.

Is It Too Late?

You may be at a point in your life at which you already have regrets. But it isn't too late. Even when we've made a mess of things, positive small changes often add up to significant benefits. And God's grace can multiply those benefits in amazing ways.

If you've spent a long time living badly, reversing your course may feel overwhelming. But remember, you didn't get where you are now in a day. It may take some time for you to realize the benefits of positive changes. Here are some examples, humanly speaking, that are manageable and within your power to change:

- If you're overweight, losing just one pound takes four pounds of pressure off your knees. Losing 10 percent of your body fat decreases your risk for diabetes, improves your cholesterol and blood pressure, and improves a woman's reproductive function.

- If you're a smoker with lung disease, quitting now will stop further deterioration and may allow significant improvement in your lung function. Your blood pressure and heart function will improve. And even after contracting lung cancer, if you quit tobacco you'll live longer.

- If your family is fragmented, eating together just twice a week will improve communication, lessen the chance of your teens getting into trouble, and probably improve your nutritional health as a bonus.

Living right prevents so much heartache in the future. Though it's never too late, it's also never too early to develop a healthy physical lifestyle, learn to handle stress wisely, manage your emotions, take responsibility for your behavior, nurture healthy relationships, and develop a strong relationship with God.

God is a God of second chances. So don't worry that it's too late. Perhaps there are some things that are permanently lost, but that doesn't mean that positive changes won't benefit you now. The message of the gospel is that you CAN begin again, from where you are right now.

Your Bucket List

Melissa was feeling "old" after having a baby at age 38. She started thinking about the rest of her life and came up with a "bucket list" of things she wanted to accomplish by the time she turned 40.

Now I'm all for having goals. But as someone who passed 40 more than 10 years ago, I can assure you that 40 isn't old! I'm well on my way to 60, and I don't know if I'll feel any older then. And I know people in their seventies who are accomplishing more than most of the rest of us who are half their age.

That said, the idea of a bucket list helps us put our lives in eternal perspective.

Here are some things you'll want to be sure you accomplish before the end of your life:

- Take a risk to love—deeply, passionately, unconditionally.

- Make sure your spouse, children, and/or other family members know you love them by your words and actions.

- Forgive those who've hurt you.

- Apologize to those you've harmed, and ask for their forgiveness.

- Fully expend your energies for the advancement of God's kingdom.

- Pass on your expertise in some skill or field to those who're coming after you.

- Live a life of integrity—not perfect, but open and clean.

- Have God fully deal with you in the areas in which you're vulnerable.

- Develop the characteristics of love, joy, peace, graciousness, kindness, faith—the "fruit of the Spirit" (Galatians 5:22,23).

One person said it like this: "Don't die with your music still in you!"

And a six-year-old girl perhaps said it best of all: "If you love someone, hurry up and show it!"

One of my professors had on his desk a plaque that read "Dr. Alexander, Eternal Medicine." It was his way of reminding himself and anyone else who came by that the choices we make today, the relationships we have, and most of all the care we give to our faith in God truly do have eternal consequences.

Suggested Discussion Questions:

1. *Do you have any regrets about things you have or haven't done at this point in your life? What regrets do you think would concern you most at the end of your life?*

2. *Do you have a "bucket list"? What would you put on it if you did?*

3. *If you could write the epitaph on your tombstone, what would it be? How do you want to be remembered?*

Suggested Action Steps:

1. *Write down your "bucket list," five to ten things you want to have completed before your life ends. Take action on one of those items this week.*

2. *With regard to what area of your life do you feel as though it may be too late? Talk to God about it, and together take one positive step in that direction this week.*

3. *If you aren't completely certain of your eternal standing with God, pray this prayer: "Dear God, I need you. I've made a mess of things. I believe Your Son Jesus died and rose again for me. Please take all of me, and change me to be who You want me to be, forever. Amen."*

Scripture to Contemplate or Memorize:

"I write these things to you who believe in the name of the Son of God so that you may know that you have eternal life." (1 John 5:13)

Closing Thoughts

I HOPE YOU'VE enjoyed sitting across from me on my little rolling stool and talking about the different areas of your life. I hope you've thought through many of the questions we've discussed and taken some action steps. And I hope you're already sensing an improved level of health in one or many areas.

As we conclude this extended consultation I want to talk to you from my heart for a moment. I don't know what brought you to read this book. Perhaps it was as assignment for your small group or from your counselor. Or perhaps you felt frustrated by some problem in your life and hoped this book would give you the answer.

Think of me sitting across from you, just the two of us, and me giving you one final takeaway.

If you're a younger person, I would put my hand on your shoulder, look you straight in the eyes, and say with all the earnestness I could display, "Don't wait! The relatively little problems you struggle with now will be so much easier to deal with while they're still small. Don't wait until later, when you'll have so many regrets. You may think your lifestyle won't catch up with you, but it will. If you need help to change, get it. But don't wait! God can do so much—in every way—with someone willing to live for Him."

And if you're an older person, I would take your hand in mine, look at you with a bit of moisture in my own eyes, and say with a heart full of compassion and hope, "It isn't too late! You may regret some of the things you've done, some of the ways you've lived. But don't give up! Today is the beginning of the rest of your life. God loves you. And He isn't finished with you. Whether it's your physical health, your family dynamic, your emotional health, your spiritual life, or anything else—there's still tomorrow. God's grace can redeem what you thought impossible. It isn't too late!"

I'd love to hear from you.

Please visit my website, drcarolministries.com.

And as we say at the close of every Dr. Carol Show, **"Now go, and live well!"**

Dr. Carol

About the Author

CAROL PETERS-TANKSLEY, MD, DMin, is a licensed medical doctor, board-certified in Obstetrics/Gynecology and Reproductive Endocrinology. For over twenty-five years she has practiced in a number of professional settings, including private practice, a medical school/university, and a large county teaching hospital. She currently practices OB-Gyn part-time, providing short-term relief for other OB-Gyn physicians and hospitals.

Dr. Carol, sometimes known as "Doctor-Doctor," is also an ordained Christian minister. In addition to her MD degree from Loma Linda University, Loma Linda, CA, she also received a Doctor of Ministry (DMin) degree from Oral Roberts University. She now spends much of her time writing and speaking about the Fully Alive life that Jesus came to give each one of us, a life characterized by good health, loving relationships, and joyful spirituality.

Dr. Carol and her husband, Al Tanksley, together hosted the Dr. Carol Show live radio program for several years until Al's death. Dr. Carol lives in Austin, Texas, where she enjoys being "Grandma Carol" to four wonderful grandchildren.

Dr. Carol would love to connect with you. Find her on her website, drcarolministries.com or @DrCarolT on the major social media networks.

Endnotes

Chapter 4

1. See her story at bethanyhamilton.com/.
2. See his story at realbencarson.com/.
3. See his story at www.hollywoodhenderson.com/.

Chapter 7

1. www.samhsa.gov/data/NSDUH/2012SummNatFindDetTables/NationalFindings/NSDUHresults2012.htm
2. www.niaaa.nih.gov/alcohol-health/overview-alcohol-consumption/alcohol-use-disorders
3. www.techaddiction.ca/files/porn-addiction-statistics.jpg
4. publicreligion.org/research/2013/04/april-2013-prri-rns-survey/
5. www.covenanteyes.com/pornstats/
6. www.celebraterecovery.com/

Chapter 8

1. Evans, Dwight, et al, "Mood Disorders in the Medically Ill: Scientific Review and Recommendations," *Biological Psychiatry* 58(3): August 2005, 175-189.
2. Kroenke, Kurt, et al, "Depressive and Anxiety Disorders in Patients Presenting With Physical Complaints," *American Journal of Medicine* 103(5): November 1997, 339-347.
3. Whooley M. A., et al, "Depressive Symptoms, Health Behaviors, and Risk of Cardiovascular Events in Patients With Coronary Heart Disease," *JAMA* 300(20): 2008, 2379-2388.
4. Edwards, B., and V. Clarke, "The psychological impact of a cancer diagnosis on families: The influence of family functioning and patients' illness characteristics on depression and anxiety," *Psycho-Oncology* 13: 2004, 562–576.
5. Gask, L., et al, "What is the relationship between diabetes and depression? A qualitative meta-synthesis of patient experience of co-morbidity," *Chronic Illness* 7(3): September 2011, 239-52.

6. Smith, J., and M. Osborn, "Pain as an assault on the self: An interpretative phenomenological analysis of the psychological impact of chronic benign low back pain," *Psychology & Health* 22(5): June 2007, 517-534.

Chapter 9

1. Meyer, Joyce. *Battlefield of the Mind*, Revised Edition. Warner Faith (New York, NY: 2002), 45.
2. psychcentral.com/lib/stress-a-cause-of-cancer/000754
3. Wolford, Chris, et al, "Transcription factor ATF3 links host adaptive response to breast cancer metastasis," *Journal of Clinical Investigation* 123(7): 2013, 2893–2906.
4. Kupper, N, et al, "Cross-cultural analysis of Type D (distressed) personality in 6222 patients with ischemic heart disease: a study from the International HeartQoL Project," *International Journal of Cardiology* 166(2): June 20 2013, 327-33.
5. Leserman, Jane, "Sexual Abuse History: Prevalence, Health Effects, Mediators, and Psychological Treatment," *Psychosomatic Medicine* 67(6): November 1 2005, 906-915.
6. Kroenke, Kurt, et al, "Anxiety Disorders in Primary Care: Prevalence, Impairment, Comorbidity, and Detection," *Annals of Internal Medicine* 146(5): March 2007, 317-325.
7. Friedberg, J. P., et al, "Relationship between forgiveness and psychological and physiological indices in cardiac patients," *International Journal of Behavioral Medicine* 16(3): March 2009, 205-11.
8. Waltman, M. A., "The effects of a forgiveness intervention on patients with coronary artery disease," *Psychology of Health* 24(1): January 2009, 11-27.
9. For some ideas on good things to think about, see my blog post at drcarolshow.com/25-good-things-to-think-about/.

Chapter 10

1. A few of my favorite electronic resources include www.christianbook.com, www.ransomedheart.com, www.crosswalk.com, and www.familylife.com. For more suggestions, check my website drcarolshow.com/helpful-links/.

Chapter 13

1. Schultz, Charles, *Peanuts*, November 12, 1959.
2. Umberson, D., and J. Montez, "Social Relationships and Health: A Flashpoint for Health Policy," *Journal of Health and Social Behavior* 51(1): November 2010, S54-S66.

Chapter 17
1. www.covenanteyes.com/pornography-facts-and-statistics/, updated February 2014.
2. Augustine of Hippo, *Confessions*.

Chapter 18
1 Kendrick, Keith M., "The Neurology of Social Bonds," *Journal of Neuroendocrinology* 16(12): December 2004, 1007–1008.

Chapter 20
1. *New York Daily News*, November 25, 2013.
2. Rosberg, Gary and Barb, *The 5 Love Needs of Men and Women*. Tyndale House Publishers, 2001.
3. www.5lovelanguages.com/
4. loveandrespect.com/

Chapter 21
1. Brizandine, Louann. *The Female Brain*. Broadway Books (New York: 2006).
2. Mehl, Mathhias R., et al, "Are Women Really More Talkative Than Men?," *Science* 317:5834: July 6 2007, 82.

Chapter 24
1. Check out www.5lovelanguages.com, or better yet, take the quiz there with your wife.
2. Every Man's Battle: newlife.com/emb/

Chapter 25
1. Pargament, Kenneth, "The Bitter and the Sweet: An Evaluation of the Costs and Benefits of Religiousness," *Psychological Inquiry* 13: 2002, 171.
2. Ibid., 177.

Chapter 26
1. A few of the many free online Bible study tools: www.biblestudytools.com/, www.biblegateway.com/, biblehub.com/
2. www.bible.com

Chapter 27
1. http://www.familylife.com/

Chapter 29

1. Ten Boom, Corrie, "I'm Still Learning To Forgive," *Guideposts* (Carmel, NY: 1972).
2. For an extensive scientific treatment of this topic, see M. E. McCullough, K. I. Pargament, and C. E. Thoresen, *Forgiveness: Theory, Research, and Practice*. The Guilford Press (New York: 2001).

Chapter 32

1. Pargament, Kenneth, "The Bitter and the Sweet: An Evaluation of the Costs and Benefits of Religiousness," *Psychological Inquiry* 13: 2002, 177.
2. ———, et al, "Religion and the Problem-Solving Process: Three Styles of Coping," *Journal for the Scientific Study of Religion* 27(1): 1988, 99.

Chapter 36

1. Ware, Bronnie. *The Top Five Regrets of the Dying: A Life Transformed by the Dearly Departing*. Hay House (Carlsbad, CA: 2012).

www.ingramcontent.com/pod-product-compliance
Lightning Source LLC
LaVergne TN
LVHW051548070426
835507LV00021B/2463